A HEART
ABLAZE

A HEART ABLAZE

IGNITING A PASSION FOR GOD

JOHN BEVERE

OLIVER
NELSON
™

THOMAS NELSON PUBLISHERS

A Division of Thomas Nelson, Inc.
www.ThomasNelson.com

Published in Nashville, Tennessee, by Thomas Nelson, Inc.

Scripture quotations noted NKJV are from THE NEW KING JAMES VERSION. Copyright © 1979, 1980, 1982, Thomas Nelson, Inc., Publishers.

Scripture quotations noted AMPLIFIED are from THE AMPLIFIED BIBLE: Old Testament. Copyright © 1962, 1964 by Zondervan Publishing House (used by permission); and from THE AMPLIFIED NEW TESTAMENT. Copyright © 1958 by the Lockman Foundation (used by permission).

Scripture quotations noted CEV are from THE CONTEMPORARY ENGLISH VERSION. © 1991 by the American Bible Society. Used by permission.

Scripture quotations noted KJV are from the KING JAMES VERSION of the Bible.

Scripture quotations noted NASB are from the NEW AMERICAN STANDARD BIBLE®. © Copyright The Lockman Foundation 1960, 1962, 1963, 1968, 1971, 1972, 1973, 1975, 1977. Used by permission.

Scripture quotations noted NCV are from The Holy Bible, New Century Version, copyright © 1987, 1988, 1991 by Word Publishing, Dallas, Texas 75234. Used by permission.

Scripture quotations noted THE MESSAGE are from The Message: The New Testament in Contemporary English. Copyright © 1993 by Eugene H. Peterson.

Scripture quotations noted NIV are from the HOLY BIBLE: NEW INTERNATIONAL VERSION®. Copyright © 1973, 1978, 1984 by International Bible Society. Used by permission of Zondervan Publishing House. All rights reserved.

Scripture quotations noted NLT are from the *Holy Bible,* New Living Translation, copyright © 1996. Used by permission of Tyndale House Publishers, Inc., Wheaton, Illinois 60189. All rights reserved.

Bevere, John.
    A heart ablaze : igniting a passion for God / John Bevere.
      p. cm.
    ISBN 0-7852-6990-8 (pbk.)
    1. Spiritual life—Christianity. I. Title.
BV4501.2.B437 1999
248.4—dc21

99-39348
CIP

Printed in the United States of America

04 05 PHX 15

I DEDICATE THIS BOOK TO TWO GODLY MEN:

FIRST, TO PASTOR AL BRICE:

You have cared for Lisa and me as if we were your own family.

You have esteemed the ministry God has entrusted to us as if He had entrusted it to you.

You have prayed for us as if you were praying for your own needs.

You have shown us a selfless love that only our Savior can give.

> Then Jonathan and David made a covenant, because he loved him as his own soul. (1 Sam. 18:3 NKJV)

Thanks, Al, you're a true friend. Almost twenty years of friendship, and we have all eternity to go!

SECOND, TO MR. LORAN JOHNSON:

You have labored with Lisa and me in this ministry and expected nothing in return.

You have rejoiced with us in victory and prayed diligently for us in our time of need.

You have loved us as a father.

> A friend is always loyal, and a brother is born to help in time of need. (Prov. 17:17 NLT)

Thanks, Loran, you're a true friend.

CONTENTS

Acknowledgments

My deepest appreciation to . . .

My wife, Lisa. Thanks for being my best friend, most faithful supporter, wife, and mother of our children. You are truly God's gift to me, and I value and treasure you. I love you, sweetheart.

Our four sons, Addison, Austin, Alexander, and Arden. All of you have brought great joy to my life. You are each a special treasure. Thank you for sharing in the call of God and encouraging me to travel and write.

My parents, John and Kay Bevere. Thank you for the godly lifestyle you live before me. You both love me not only in word but also by your actions.

Pastor Al Brice, Loran Johnson, Rob Birkbeck, Tony Stone, and Steve Watson. Thank you for serving on the advisory board of our United States and European ministry offices. The love, kindness, and wisdom you have selflessly given have touched and strengthened our hearts.

The staff of John Bevere Ministries. Thank you for your unwavering support and faithfulness. Lisa and I love each of you.

David and Pam Graham. Thank you for your sincere and faithful support in overseeing the operations of our European office.

Our new pastor, Ted Haggard. Your enthusiasm and joy over our family and ministry have been a great encouragement to us. We look forward to the years ahead.

Rory and Wendy Alec. Thanks for believing in the message God has placed in our heart. We treasure your friendship.

Victor Oliver, Rolf Zettersten, and Michael Hyatt. Thanks for your encouragement and belief in the message God has burned in our hearts.

Brian Hampton. Thank you for your editing skills in this project. But most of all thanks for your support.

All the staff of Thomas Nelson Publishers. Thanks for the support of this message and for your professional and kind help. You are a great group to work with.

Most important, my sincere gratitude to my Lord. How can words adequately acknowledge all You have done for me and for Your people? I love You more than I am able to express.

INTRODUCTION

This book is a journey toward truth. Many long for truth, yet when confronted by it, they reject, ignore, or twist it for their own benefit. This condition has created desperate problems for our generation, resulting in a society bathed in deception. Jesus repeatedly warned the children of our day against this very thing.

Deception poses a major problem because those in its grip believe they are walking in truth. Paul described the latter days to Timothy: "For the time will come when they will not endure sound doctrine, but according to their own desires, because they have itching ears, they will heap up for themselves teachers; and they will turn their ears away from the truth, and be turned aside to fables" (2 Tim. 4:3–4 NKJV). One definition of the Greek word for *fables* in verse 4 is "falsehood." If falsehood is represented as truth long enough, many will stand by it with their very lives.

When the actual truth is revealed through Scriptures, it will be rejected as heresy. Paul warned that they will not endure sound doctrine. I heard one speaker say, "Unsound doctrines taught in our churches are not messages from the phone book. They are messages taught from Scriptures." He was warning that these are doctrines derived from the Bible and therefore widely accepted, even though they are unsound.

The writer of Proverbs foresaw this situation and wrote, "There is a generation that is pure in its own eyes, yet is not washed from its filthiness" (Prov. 30:12 NKJV). We will learn through this book that the generation is ours.

If truth was pleasant to our senses and easy to embrace, the entire world would knock at its door and enter. However, Jesus made it clear that is not the case: "Everyone practicing evil hates the light and does not come to the light, lest his deeds should be exposed. But he who does the truth comes to the light, that his deeds may be clearly seen, that they have been done in God" (John 3:20–21 NKJV). Only those who fear God love truth.

This day and this hour bring with them difficult questions. Why do so many in the church lack passion? We've invested billions of dollars in media, buildings, advertisements, and countless other venues to propagate the gospel, yet why do so many in the church still wrestle with lust and the desire for the pleasures of this world? Why do more than 80 percent of our converts wander back into a world of darkness? How can sinners claim a new birth experience yet remain unchanged? I believe an answer to all of the above can be found in: a lack of the fire and passion of God.

If we look at those who went before us, we find clear differences. What gave Moses the desire to pursue God when it cost him a lifetime of achievements? Why did Jeremiah, Isaiah, and others continue to proclaim the very words that brought them persecution and hardship? Why were people in the early church able to forsake their possessions, comfort, and very lives for the gospel? What strength did the early church possess that enabled them to boldly preach under the threat of torture and death when the greatest struggle for too many in the church today is overcoming a bad self-image? Again, the answer is the fire of God.

We need the fire of God, and it is available to one and all who hunger for truth. It does not come without confrontation, but most are already fed up with flattery and are ready for change. The fear of remaining the same outweighs any painful encounter with truth. Those who take such a position are desperate to hear from the Lord of glory. They are ready to see Him truly glorified in their lives.

No matter where you are in your walk with God, there is still room for more of His holy fire. If you fear the fire is almost gone, take courage and have hope. He has already promised:

INTRODUCTION

A bruised reed He will not break,
And smoking flax He will not quench,
Till He sends forth justice to victory. (Matt. 12:20 NKJV)

What gracious love our Father has! I pray that this book will progressively reveal His true concern for our condition. He is more concerned with our condition than our comfort and loves us enough to tell us what we need to hear.

I have never been so excited about a message because these truths have touched me deeply. This project only strengthened the realization of the One who truly authored it. I am only a vessel through whom the Master has spoken His message. I am careful to give Him all the glory for whatever He does through this book. May it ignite a holy fire in your life, and may you never be the same. As we begin this journey, let's pray,

Father, in the name of Jesus, as I read this book, I ask that You would speak to me personally by Your Spirit. I am not afraid of truth. I desire it. As I embrace it, cause Your holy fire to burn within my heart. Let its intensity consume me, causing me to love what You love and hate what You hate. As I read, open my eyes to see Jesus more clearly than ever before. I acknowledge that He is the revealed Word of God and the Truth. I thank You in advance for changing my life by Your message within this book. Amen.

CHAPTER 1

AN UNFORGETTABLE EVENING

God will ignite His people with an intense, burning
passion like we have never known before.

It was the fourth and final in a series of meetings at Covenant Love Family Church, Fayetteville, North Carolina. It was not my first time with them, for I had ministered at this church several times before. The meetings always bore wonderful fruit because of their genuine hunger and love for God.

It was late, long past the time a regular service would have let out. Yet I was hesitant to close; I was in the midst of a struggle. The message had come forth clear and concise, and the people had responded enthusiastically. But I felt a sense of incompleteness. I was usually able to close a series of services with a sense of fulfillment, especially with such a receptive church. That night it was different.

Adding to this struggle, I kept hearing the words the Holy Spirit whispered in my heart while I was flying to Fayetteville: "These meetings will be the most powerful you have experienced at this church."

I had been to this church seven or eight times over the years, and I wouldn't hesitate to include it on my list of the most life-changing meetings. I remember thinking on the plane: *That's saying a lot.*

As I stood on the platform, I was bewildered. The meetings were not the most powerful. It was hard for me not to compare them to the significant acts and testimonies in previous services. I wrestled with the temptation of complaining within, yet I knew I had to stay focused on the service before me. I desperately needed to hear from God.

It seemed the presence of God was hovering over the people. It was almost as if He wanted to fall on the congregation in a strong and powerful way, yet was somehow restrained. There were isolated pockets of people weeping here and there, but I knew God wanted much more. Although I had sensed a similar atmosphere on previous nights, I was certain that on the last night the Lord would honor us with His refreshing presence, just as He had in the past. There was not to be another service. "Why is He not touching these people when I perceive He desires to?" I kept asking myself.

REVELATION THAT GAVE DIRECTION

Then I heard the still, small voice of the Holy Spirit speak to me. He showed me that something was hindering the churches of this city, just as there was a hindrance in the service. It kept the churches from growing beyond a certain point. Once they achieved it, they either split or became religious and ineffective.

No sooner had I shared this with the congregation than the pastor jumped up and confirmed it. He had done present and historical studies on the city and affirmed this was statistically correct. While he was speaking I again heard the voice of the Holy Spirit. He explained how this hindrance could be broken.

When the pastor was finished speaking, he handed the microphone back to me. I said, "Folks, God has shown me that a forty-day fast will break this hindrance."

I could almost hear the thoughts of the people, *Go forty days without food!*

I continued, "It is not necessarily a food fast, and most likely it is not a total refraining from food. It is a fast of what keeps you from seeking the Lord. It may be television, videos, computer games, newspapers, excessive shopping and phone conversations, and so forth."

This is a true fast. Too often we go on hunger strikes to hear from God, yet continue our busy, distracted lives. That is not a fast; therefore, we get very little benefit. A true fast occurs when we abstain for the purpose of seeking God in a more focused manner.

The children of Israel would abstain from food and question the Lord: "Why aren't You impressed?" or "Why don't You even notice our efforts?"

God answered them through the prophet Isaiah, "I will tell you why! It's because you are living for yourselves even while you are fasting . . . This kind of fasting will never get you anywhere with me" (Isa. 58:3–4 NLT).

I returned the microphone to the pastor, and he immediately committed himself to the fast and pleaded with the entire congregation to do the same. They set their hearts as one to seek God.

The next day I realized the Sunday forty days later was open in my schedule. I shared this with the pastor, and he responded, "I would love for you to be here."

Over the following weeks we kept in touch. Already exciting testimonies were coming from the families who were fasting. Students, who previously struggled in school, were seeing their C's and D's rise to A's and B's. There were reports of increased obedience and respect in children and teenagers. Worldly things and pursuits seemed to be losing their hold and attraction. Wives excitedly shared how their husbands were like different men. Fathers were leading Bible studies and praying with their families. Relationships were healed while still others were experiencing physical healing. Homes were turning around as people drew near to God.

I also learned from the pastor how their services were increasingly more powerful with several new people coming into the kingdom of

God. Virtually all areas were being affected as a result of this church's obedience to heed the word of the Lord.

A Day I Will Never Forget

Six Sundays later, November 3, 1996, I returned to the church to minister. It would be a day I'd never forget. Even as I entered the sanctuary for the morning service, I noticed the air was thick with expectancy. The message I gave from the Word of God was met with absorbent hearts and souls.

At the conclusion of the service the pastor exhorted the congregation to arrive early that evening to prepare their hearts in prayer. He also instructed the parents that children's church would be included in the main service that evening; he wanted all age-groups together for that service with the exception of those ages six and under. I had never known him to do that before. He admonished the parents, "If you or your children miss this service, you will regret it the rest of your life." His comment surprised and almost concerned me, but I elected not to say anything, and I'm glad I didn't.

That night the auditorium was packed with nearly 1,300 people. I taught on the fear of the Lord, with the message concluding at approximately 9:00 P.M. The teaching was so intense, you could have heard a pin drop in the auditorium anytime I paused, even with all the young children in attendance.

At the conclusion of the message, the worship leader and I led the congregation in a couple of worship songs. I then heard the Spirit of God whisper, "I want to minister to the people. Please allow Me to."

I realized that even though we were singing songs of worship, it was not the direction He desired. I alerted the people, "The Lord just spoke to my heart. He wants to minister to us, so let's be still and focus on Him."

For the next ten minutes or so, you could hear various people crying quietly in the presence of the Lord. From all appearances it seemed the same as the services six weeks earlier, yet I knew something was different and about to happen.

About 9:15 the quiet atmosphere suddenly changed. From the back of the building I could hear high-pitched cries. It was easy to identify them as the voices of the youngsters. Approximately 150 children who were ages seven through twelve were sitting with their teachers in the back right-hand side of the auditorium. I knew God was touching them. I invited them forward by saying, "The children, God is touching the children. I want all the children that God is touching to come down to the front of the platform."

I will never forget what I saw. Some of you may think what I share is a bit extreme, and if I had not seen it, along with 1,200 other witnesses in attendance, I might agree. Frankly I will not be able to do it justice when I describe the magnitude of what God did that night, but I will make an attempt. I want to point out that it is a fairly conservative church. Most of the members are from denominational backgrounds that are not demonstrative, or they have not grown up in church at all and have been saved in this church. The pastor is a very good teacher and not given to extremism, sensationalism, or hype.

I observed children, mostly ages seven through nine years, coming down the aisle toward me, weeping uncontrollably. Many covered their faces with their hands. Others struggled to walk straight. Upon reaching the platform area, some fell to their knees because they lacked the strength to stand, but most collapsed as if their knees completely gave way. They fell all over, some on top of one another. The teary-eyed ushers helped them. Within moments, I watched as nearly one hundred small children wept and cried, while most shook profusely. They were engulfed in the manifested presence of the Lord.

This did not go on for two or three minutes; it lasted more than an hour! You would think hearing so many children weep and wail for such a long period of time would possibly be irritating, but it was glorious. Most of the adults' eyes were filled with tears as they watched what God was doing in the children. Yet at the same time they themselves were being strongly touched by the powerful presence of God. It was as if one wave of God's presence would come in only to be followed by another one more powerful. When it seemed that the children couldn't cry, scream, or shake any longer, another wave of God's presence would come and raise the intensity to another level. At times I could only drop my head on the podium because of the heaviness of God's presence.

I watched one young girl, no more than seven years old, wring her hands profusely as though they were on fire. Her uplifted face was bathed in tears as she cried out. You could sense God on these children so strongly that the ushers did not touch them after initially helping them. They just stood, watched, and cried.

Several adults lay on their faces—motionless. Others stood watching in awe through eyes blurred by tears. Several times I looked behind me and saw the pastor with his face in his hands, weeping. His wife had collapsed in tears in the choir loft.

Later the pastor wrote a letter describing the evening from his vantage point. Though his account is similar, I felt it was important as another perspective.

Sunday, November 3, 1996, will be a day I will never forget. I believe it foreshadows what God is about to do in the earth. John ministered in the evening service on the fear of the Lord then declared, "We must let Jesus be Master in every area of our lives and we must now completely surrender to Him as our Lord."

We worshipped for a short while, then John said, "I sense the Holy Spirit moving now in this place." At this point, I heard sobs rise from the children, youth and adults. Adults began to come to the altar weeping and sobbing. John then said, "God is touching the children, the children are going to be touched powerfully by the Lord." He then encouraged the children who were being touched by God's presence to come.

I saw children run to the altar weeping uncontrollably: this included my sons [3] and daughter, all over children on their faces and knees called and screamed out to Jesus. Some shook and wrung their hands profusely as the fire of God moved in their midst. Nearly a hundred crowded the altars, while waves of God's Spirit shot through the sanctuary. I watched as one child after another fell on top of each other, no one had touched them. They looked like dominoes. For an hour and a half [it was an hour and fifteen minutes but I did not want to change what he wrote], we were saturated by God's presence. Near the end of the service parents and children embraced and wept as God knit their hearts.

One ten year old told us, as he lay on the floor, he saw rays of brilliant white light shooting down from the ceiling and falling on everyone. Several adults in the congregation and choir repeated the same thing. No one left service until 11:00 P.M. Children were carried out as they still wept.

I am still receiving reports of changed families; children are witnessing and obeying, etc. As pastor I can truly say my home and children are different.

> Dr. Al Brice, Senior Pastor
> Covenant Love Family Church
> Fayetteville, North Carolina

The report given by the young man who saw the brilliant rays of white light shooting down from the ceiling got my attention. In the book of Habakkuk, we read,

> LORD, I have heard of your fame;
>   I stand in awe of your deeds, O LORD.
> Renew them in our day,
>   in our time make them known;
>   in wrath remember mercy.
> God came from Teman,
>   the Holy One from Mount Paran. Selah

> His glory covered the heavens
> > and his praise filled the earth.
> His splendor was like the sunrise;
> > rays flashed from his hand,
> > > where his power was hidden. (Hab. 3:2–4 NIV)

I'm sure this young man had no idea that Habakkuk recorded anything like this so long ago. With our eyes, we witnessed what Joel had prophesied, "Your sons and daughters will prophesy, . . . your young men will see visions" (2:28 NIV). The ten-year-old was describing a similar vision already described in Scripture without prior knowledge.

Another boy proclaimed with boldness, "Mom, the fast isn't over." Not only were his words prophetic, but he verbalized the desire of numerous others. These young people had experienced the presence of the living God, and their lives were changed. They wanted to press on and not stop.

Later that night the pastor's wife shared with us the Scriptures God had spoken to her about what had transpired:

> Therefore also now, says the Lord, turn and keep on coming to Me with all your heart, with fasting, with weeping, and with mourning [until every hindrance is removed and the broken fellowship is restored]. Rend your hearts and not your garments. (Joel 2:12–13 AMPLIFIED)

As she read these verses, my heart burned within. The phrase "keep on coming" described that church's resolve. The people were set in their pursuit of His heart. They would not draw back.

God instructs us to rend our hearts and not our garments. I have seen believers and churches that by appearance seem to have it all together, yet not touch the heart of God as this church had. The reason? They may fast, hold prayer meetings, and abstain from outward indulgences, causing them to look good as far as the outward "garment" is concerned, but inwardly they conceal stubborn hearts. They still live for their own agendas rather than for the service of others. God is more impressed with inward submission than outward appearances of Christianity. Joel continued,

> Blow the trumpet in Zion,
>> declare a holy fast,
>> call a sacred assembly.
> Gather the people,
>> consecrate the assembly;
>> bring together the elders,
>> gather the children,
>> those nursing at the breast.
> Let the bridegroom leave his room
>> and the bride her chamber. (Joel 2:15–16 NIV)

The fire in my heart spread as she continued to read. It described exactly how God had instructed this church just forty days earlier. When the prophetic word was trumpeted, everyone was to seek God. From the leaders to the children, no one was exempt. Continuing, she read,

> And it shall come to pass afterward
> That I will pour out My Spirit on all flesh;
> Your sons and your daughters shall prophesy,
> Your old men shall dream dreams,
> Your young men shall see visions.
> And also on My menservants and on My maidservants
> I will pour out My Spirit in those days. (Joel 2:28–29 NKJV)

"And it shall come to pass afterward." I have heard this verse quoted repeatedly. In fact, since I was first saved, Joel 2:28–29 has been frequently referenced by believers and ministers alike. There is talk of sons and daughters prophesying and seeing visions along with the great wonders and signs of the Holy Spirit, yet often the word afterward was ignored in the discussions and preaching. If something is prophesied to happen afterward, then something significant must take place before-ward: the church's response to the trumpet, by drawing near to God.

God responds powerfully when we draw near. We must come close when He calls. Another important element is timing. This is where many believers miss it. I believe as you read this book, you'll realize that though believers have an open invitation to come to the Lord through prayer and fellowship at any time, there are times and seasons when He calls us for specific purposes. During these, timing becomes crucial, for if we do not respond, we will miss the blessing He desires to give us.

The focus in these times is on obedience rather than our own will or desire. God is much more pleased with obedience than sacrifice. I have seen churches that fast regularly and pray around the clock with precious members sacrificing sleep to fill their prayer slots. Yet this does not guarantee His power and presence. Too often I have seen these churches lack what the church I wrote about had in abundance. They had the form; they just did not have the heart.

It is the same with individuals. I have seen many who fast and pray religiously, yet they lack the liberty, power, and intimate knowledge of God that I have seen in others who have not sacrificed nearly as much, but responded to the Spirit of God's leading.

The church heeded the calling voice of God. In the next year and a half they doubled in size. In fact, they had just finished building the auditorium that we met in that night, and within six months they had to start another building program for a larger sanctuary.

The pastor and I spoke frequently for months afterward. He said, "John, our Sunday morning second service, which starts at 10:00 A.M., keeps getting out between two and three o'clock in the afternoon." One Sunday he called and said that he had to tell the people, "Please, go home." He said they just stood there looking at him, not wanting to leave.

God fulfilled His word. Those meetings were the most powerful we had experienced. Through our cooperation with His Spirit and our obedience to His leading, He had His way. Three years have passed, yet the pastor still receives reports from that service. The fruit has remained. I have ministered there several times since and have seen only an increase of passion and genuine hunger for God.

A Foretaste of What's Coming

A year earlier, I was in Kuala Lumpur, Malaysia, ministering in the nation's largest Bible school for a week of services. At our eighth service, there was a very similar experience, but this one lasted only about five to ten minutes. God's Spirit fell on the students and many others in attendance. It is another meeting I will never forget. The morning after the service while I was in prayer, God spoke to me, "What you saw yesterday, you will see happening all over, for it is one of the final moves of My Spirit, which will occur in the church." He showed me how this move of His Spirit would yield the fruit of true holiness in the church and prepare it for the harvest to come. God will ignite His people with an intense, burning passion like we have never known before.

I do not believe you hold this book by chance; rather, by divine providence you have it to create a hunger and prepare your heart for what He is about to do. We must ready ourselves for His second coming. The apostle John recorded: "Let us be glad and rejoice and give Him glory, for the marriage of the Lamb has come, and His wife has made herself ready" (Rev. 19:7 NKJV).

We are that bride of Christ, and we have a crucial role in making ourselves ready to be united with Him. I want to reemphasize this point: we are to make ourselves ready. It is a divine merger. He does not do all of it for us! It is our response to His provision. He provides the grace, and we embrace the fire. He is not coming back for a church spotted and blemished by the world. He will return for a pure bride whose heart is ablaze with true holiness.

CHAPTER 2

THE PURPOSE OF SALVATION

God, who created the universe and everything within it, expresses
His intent to dwell in us and among us.

I have frequently heard leaders use the word *visitation* when describing an encounter with God's presence, whether it was on a corporate basis, such as the church service described in the last chapter, or on an individual basis. The Lord's desire is not a *visitation;* rather, He seeks a *habitation*. Let me illustrate the difference: I have neighbors who are good friends, and on numerous occasions I have gone to their homes to spend time with them. But once the visit is over I return to my house, which is my dwelling place. One of the greatest promises the Lord makes to believers is this:

> I will dwell in them
> And walk among them.
> I will be their God,
> And they shall be My people. (2 Cor. 6:16 NKJV)

What a statement! God, who created the universe and all that is within it, expresses His intent to dwell in and among us. In accordance with this promise, Paul writes that we "are being built together for a dwelling place of God in the Spirit" (Eph. 2:22 NKJV).

These are His promises to us. However, every promise in the Bible is conditional, and if the condition is not met, the promise is made ineffective, not by God's unfaithfulness, but by our own. It is impossible for God to lie, but not impossible for man to nullify His word (Mark 7:13) by ignoring it or twisting it. This also includes the promise of God dwelling in us and among us.

Paul goes on,

> Come out from among them
> And be separate, says the Lord.
> Do not touch what is unclean,
> And I will receive you. (2 Cor. 6:17 NKJV)

The condition is that we would come out from the world's system. If we meet this condition, God says He will receive us. Conversely, if we do not come out, He will not receive us. Why will He not receive us? To answer, we must have the understanding that God is pure light and in Him is not a trace of darkness. Darkness cannot abide in the presence of pure light.

We will see as we progress in this message that His light speaks of His holiness. The Bible does not say that He *has* holiness; it says that He *is* holy (Lev. 19:2)! The world's system is darkness, and those who are drawn to darkness cannot abide in the light.

God declares, "So set yourselves apart to be holy, for I, the LORD, am your God" (Lev. 20:7 NLT). To set ourselves apart is to refuse a relationship with the world. James clearly states to us in the new covenant, "If your aim is to enjoy this world, you can't be a friend of God" (James 4:4 NLT). Another version is even blunter: "Anyone who chooses to be a friend of the world becomes an enemy of God" (NIV).

Peter emphasizes God's desire for a pure people by writing, "But now you must be holy in everything you do, just as God—who chose you to be his children—is holy. For he himself has said, 'You must be holy because I am holy'" (1 Peter 1:15–16 NLT). Being holy is not an option. God will not dwell in us and among us if we fail to heed His condition of separating ourselves from the world's system. A contemporary version reads,

> "So leave the corruption and compromise;
>> leave it for good," says God.
> "Don't link up with those who will pollute you.
> I want you all for myself." (2 Cor. 6:17 THE MESSAGE)

The magnitude of God's promises to be our Father and dwell in us and among us makes it even more important for us to carefully consider the condition He places on them. Taking into consideration the seriousness of this condition, Paul stated, "Therefore, having these promises, beloved, let us cleanse ourselves from all filthiness of the flesh and spirit, perfecting holiness in the fear of God" (2 Cor. 7:1 NKJV).

Those verses hold so much meaning that volumes could be written about them. But most believers' understanding of what is being said is limited. Many do not comprehend it at all because they do not understand the context. Paul is quoting what God spoke to Israel in the Old Testament, and by doing that he is also making known that His wishes have not changed toward us in the New. We need to understand the situations and events that led up to these statements. When we have this background, the words have the spiritual impact He intended them to have.

Consider a movie in which the writers, director, and actors have carefully designed a plot that builds up to a climactic scene at the end. Much has transpired to bring you to this point, and after walking through all the drama that led up to the climactic scene, you are overwhelmed. If you heard the actor make the same statement without seeing all the drama beforehand, it would have very little, if any, impact.

I experienced this as a young man. I walked into our family room where my sisters and parents were watching a movie. They were captivated by the story and would not be interrupted. Most of them didn't realize I had walked into the room. I glanced toward the screen at the moment the lead actor made what seemed to be a dramatic statement. My sisters began to cry. But his statement meant little to me. I thought, *What's the big deal?* I was oblivious to what was happening; yet his words riveted them and evoked deep emotion.

The same principle applies here. Many believers come to these climactic words from God's mouth and read right over them because they have not understood the drama leading up to them. To really experience the impact of what God is saying to us, we must understand the story line or drama leading up to these statements. This will take several chapters to develop. To begin, we need to go to the book of Exodus.

I WILL TURN ASIDE TO SEE

The book of Exodus opens with Abraham's descendants in captivity. They had been in Egypt for almost four hundred years. The beginning of their stay was favorable, but as time passed, they became slaves and were brutally mistreated.

Moses, a Hebrew-born man, escaped the harsh treatment; he was brought into Pharaoh's house as a babe and raised as his grandson. When he was forty years of age, however, Moses was forced to flee to another land from the wrath of Pharaoh because of his loyalty to his own people.

Forty years later while he was in the back side of the desert tending his father-in-law's flocks, God revealed Himself to Moses. The revelation occurred at Mount Sinai, which is called Horeb, the Mountain of God. The Lord appeared to him in a flame of fire from the midst of a bush. When Moses saw the bush burning with fire, yet not consumed, he said, "'I will now turn aside and see this great sight, why the bush does not burn.' So when the LORD saw that he turned aside to look, God called to him from the midst of the bush" (Ex. 3:3–4 NKJV).

It was not until Moses turned aside to draw near to the Lord's presence that anything transpired between him and God. Once God saw that Moses left his intended course of personal business to draw near, the Lord called to him and proceeded to reveal Himself to Moses through His word. If Moses had carelessly neglected it as a thing not worth noticing, God probably would have departed and said nothing to him. We are admonished in the New Testament to "draw near to God and He will draw near to [us]" (James 4:8 NKJV).

Who draws near first? God or us? God woos us, but it is not until we first draw near to God that He in turn draws near to us for the purpose of revealing Himself. This is the message of this book. In fact, this is the focus of our destiny.

THE PURPOSE OF GOD'S DELIVERANCE

God revealed Himself to Moses and told him to take His words to Pharaoh to let His people go. Despite Pharaoh's stubbornness and strength, God delivered the descendants of Abraham with a mighty hand of miracles, signs, and wonders.

Israel's deliverance from Egyptian bondage correlates to our deliverance from the slavery of sin in the New Testament. Egypt is a type of the world's system, and Israel is a type of the church. When we were born again, we were set free from the world's system of tyranny and oppression.

Where was Moses headed with the children of Israel after they were liberated? When I ask this question publicly in services, people usually respond, "To the promised land."

Yet that is not true. He was headed for Mount Horeb, or Sinai. God's words to Pharaoh, through Moses, were: "Let my people go, so that they may worship me in the desert" (Ex. 7:16; 8:1, 20; 9:1, 13; 10:3 NIV). Why would Moses want to take the people into the promised land without first meeting the Promiser? The Lord would not desire that for His people. If they were taken into the promised land without the revelation of God, they would make it into a place of idolatry.

This is what has happened with too many in the church who have been saved in the past twenty-five years. The emphasis has been on communicating God's promises and provisions, rather than His character and nature, to draw people to Him. Our messages have attracted people to a better lifestyle accompanied by eternal security instead of drawing them to know and serve the Lord of glory. Many ministers are careful to deliver a positive message that will attract the multitudes; they forgo a strong, reproving message that will bring the changes we need to face a holy God.

Meeting God at Sinai had changed Moses, and he knew that a similar experience was essential for the people. Had he not encountered the Lord at the burning bush, he would have been on a campaign to get them out of slavery into their own land, which he was attempting to do in his earlier years and caused him to flee from Pharaoh.

Many have been saved today because of ministers' messages proclaimed out of their calls rather than the revelation of God. If we have a calling on our lives but have not allowed God to bring us to the back side of His desert to reveal Himself, we will seek to free people for the sake of freedom. But we need to free people for the purpose of coming to the One for whom we were created.

In the book of Acts, we read that

> Moses was learned in all the wisdom of the Egyptians, and was mighty in words and deeds. Now when he was forty years old, it came into his heart to visit his brethren, the children of Israel. And seeing one of them suffer wrong, he defended and avenged him who

was oppressed, and struck down the Egyptian. For he supposed that his brethren would have understood that God would deliver them by his hand. (Acts 7:22–25 NKJV)

Moses saw the suffering and desired to alleviate it. He also knew he was called to deliver God's people. It was in his heart. Yet without the revelation of God he was not prepared to lead them to their destiny. Leadership without the right purpose can be more dangerous than no leadership at all. Moses was a leader, he had a purpose, but his purpose was incomplete. Without the revelation of God he could lead them at best to a land of provision void of the real purpose of their freedom—the intimate knowledge of God. That was why God led him to the back parts of His desert to quiet Moses' heart from the world he had left. In the desert he could respond with desire to God's revelation. The preparation enabled him to say, "I will now turn aside and see . . ."

We must realize that not all "good" is true ministry. At forty years of age, Moses' wanting to see his people free was good, but it was not true ministry. Eve was drawn to the "good" side of the tree of the knowledge of good and evil, not the evil side. When she "saw that the fruit of the tree was good . . . and pleasing to the eye, and also desirable for gaining wisdom, she took some and ate it" (Gen. 3:6 NIV). She was tempted to be like God. There is much that appears to be good and like God, yet is against His character and nature. Only when we come into intimate knowledge of Him can we truly discern what is good.

BROUGHT YOU TO MYSELF

Moses led the people of God out of Egypt to take them to worship God in the desert. Yet they did not immediately go to Sinai. It took them three months to make a journey that could have been made in ten or eleven days. Why did God do that? The answer is simple and was no different from the situation with Moses: God wanted to give them time to quiet their hearts so that they would embrace the revelation of God as Moses did.

Once they arrived at the foot of Mount Sinai, Moses left the people there and ascended to where God's presence was. Then the Lord called to him from the mountain, saying: "Thus you shall say to the house of Jacob, and tell the children of Israel . . ." (Ex. 19:3 NKJV).

Before we read more of what God said to Moses, I must point out to whom the message was addressed. It was not just to Aaron and his sons. It was not just to the sons of Levi. God's message was to the entire nation of Israel. It was for every person who was delivered out of Egypt, from the least to the greatest of tribes, families, and persons.

Now hear God's message: "You have seen what I did to the Egyptians, and how I bore you on eagles' wings and brought you to Myself" (Ex. 19:4 NKJV). The phrase, "and brought you to Myself," tells the whole reason you were created! The motive for which God brought you forth and went to great lengths to save you was to bring you to Himself!

We see this motive from the beginning of mankind. Why did God put man in the Garden? Adam was not created to have a worldwide deliverance ministry. He was not placed in the Garden to build bridges or skyscrapers. No, he was placed in the Garden to walk in fellowship with the living God. Out of that fellowship may emerge skyscrapers or ministry, but that is not His purpose for man's existence.

The first seven years after I was saved, I attended and eventually worked for a large church that emphasized God's promises and provisions. It was a very evangelistic church with a passion to reach the world with the good news of the gospel, yet the gospel preached there accented the benefits of the kingdom rather than the glory of knowing God. People traveled from all over the world to come to the congregation, for it was well known internationally. The leader's zeal to see others saved was contagious. Many people in the international outreach church had a passion for ministry, and I was certainly one of them.

In those first few years of my association with that church I arose each morning and prayed as long as an hour and a half before going to work. I asked God to use me to reach the lost and dying, to heal the sick. I cried out to go to the nations to set the captives free. On and on I prayed fervently till one morning I heard the Lord say to my heart, "John, your prayers are off!"

I thought to myself, *That can't be God's voice. That has to be the enemy.* Yet I knew it was the voice of the Lord. I was bewildered: "Lord, how can You say this to me? I am praying for people to be saved, healed, and delivered. This is what You desire!" But God saw beyond my words. He saw how little I knew of His true nature, and without it He knew that even though I would have been leading people out of bondage, such ministry would have eventually led me and many of those I taught to further bondage of idolatry—within the church setting.

He said to me, "John, the goal of Christianity is not ministry. You can cast out demons, heal the sick, and lead people to salvation, yet end up in hell." He added, "Judas left his job to follow Me, he healed the sick, he raised the dead, and he cast out demons, yet he is in hell." Those words riveted my heart.

We have to remember that when the apostles went out with power to heal the sick, raise the dead, and cast out devils, Judas was included (Matt. 10:1–8).

I quickly asked, "Then what is the goal of Christianity?"

He immediately replied, "To know Me intimately!" I then remembered that Paul said he counted all things as rubbish that he "may know Him" (Phil. 3:10 NKJV).

The Lord whispered to my heart, "Out of that intimate relationship will come true ministry." Daniel confirmed that by saying, "But the people who know their God shall be strong, and carry out great exploits" (Dan. 11:32 NKJV).

Jesus asserts that the blind will lead the blind into a ditch (Matt. 15:14). This is true for all who seek to lead people out of captivity without first having their eyes open to see the Lord. That is why Paul so earnestly prayed that the eyes of our hearts would be enlightened in the knowledge of Him (Eph. 1:18). It is in His light that we see (Ps. 36:9). Without a revelation of Him we are blind. Those who have not come to intimately know Him may have good motives, but without the revelation of God, they will eventually lead others into the same ditch that they themselves are heading into.

That happened during my early years of Christianity. The pastor kept his eyes more on the blessings of the covenant rather than the Blesser. He led a very elaborate lifestyle that was obtained from believing and acting on the covenant promises of God, yet he was void of the revelation of God's character and began to drift into error. He eventually stood before his congregation and stated that he did not want to live any longer with his wife who bore his children. He told the people if they did not approve, they could leave. He then married a young, energetic, and ambitious woman who was in ministry as well. She became a great snare to his life. His church dwindled from thousands to hundreds, with many shipwrecked and out of the church. He eventually divorced again and sold the church to the city.

Moses knew what had transformed his life: his encounter and intimate fellowship with the living God. He knew where to lead the people. It was not directly to the promises; it was to the only One who would truly satisfy. He recognized his purpose for being created and realized the need to find the heart of God. His heart was not revealed in God's hand of blessing; it was revealed from hearing God's words face-to-face.

CHAPTER 3

GETTING EGYPT OUT

Our responsibility as a church has been to consecrate ourselves for the past two thousand years in preparation for His coming!

God's purpose for delivering the children of Israel out of Egyptian bondage was to bring them to Himself so that He might dwell among them. We see this in His words spoken to Moses: "And they shall know that I am the LORD their God, who brought them up out of the land of Egypt, that I may dwell among them" (Ex. 29:46 NKJV). Remember, He was seeking not a visitation, but a habitation.

Now consider the words of Peter in the New Testament (read them carefully): "Coming to Him as to a living stone, rejected indeed by men, but chosen by God and precious, you also, as living stones, are being built up a spiritual house, a holy priesthood, to offer up spiritual sacrifices acceptable to God through Jesus Christ" (1 Peter 2:4–5 NKJV). God desires a dwelling place, which Peter calls His spiritual house. We are living building blocks of this abode in which God Himself desires to abide.

Peter links our role as God's dwelling place with priesthood. Why does he link the two together? As human beings, only priests may come close to God without coming under judgment. Of the numerous definitions of a priest, the one that stands above all is that a priest can come near to God to minister to Him (Ezek. 44:13, 15). To come near Him is certainly a requirement for us to be His dwelling place. We must be able to stand in His holy, awesome presence.

Turning again to 1 Peter, we read,

> Therefore it is also contained in the Scripture,
> "Behold, I lay in Zion
> A chief cornerstone, elect, precious,
> And he who believes on Him will by no means be put to shame."
> Therefore, to you who believe, He is precious; but to those
> who are disobedient,
> "The stone which the builders rejected
> Has become the chief cornerstone,"
> and
> "A stone of stumbling
> And a rock of offense."
> They stumble, being disobedient to the word, to which they also
> were appointed. (1 Peter 2:6–8 NKJV)

A peculiar statement appears in these verses. Peter says, "To you who believe . . . but to those who are disobedient." He contrasts the words *believe* and *disobey*. We cannot do that today. Currently, the word *believe* has nothing to do with obedience or disobedience. That is why many within the church do not emphasize obedience. However, in the days of the New Testament writers they were closely connected. To believe meant not only to acknowledge His existence but also to obey. In other words, if you believed, you obeyed, and the evidence of not believing was a disobedient lifestyle. Paul writes that Jesus, "having been perfected, . . . became the author of eternal salvation to all who obey Him" (Heb. 5:9 NKJV).

Obedience is a crucial element of salvation. Jesus Himself notes that there will be a multitude who will believe on Him and call Him Lord, and even do miracles in His name, yet they will be denied entrance into the kingdom of God because they did not do or obey the will of God (Matt. 7:21).

A Royal Priesthood Called into His Marvelous Light

The children of Israel stumbled or fell short of what they were called to; they were disobedient to the word to which they were appointed. But then Peter goes on to say of us: "But you are a chosen generation, a royal priesthood, a holy nation, His own special people, that you may proclaim the praises of Him who called you out of darkness into His marvelous light" (1 Peter 2:9 NKJV).

We are a royal priesthood and a holy nation. God is the King; He is royalty. Therefore, those who come near to minister to Him must be royal priests, for only royalty can minister to and fellowship with royalty!

Those who are His priests have been called out of darkness into His marvelous light—not just light, but marvelous light! We have diminished and become overfamiliar with a few English words used to describe God's greatness. *Marvelous* is certainly one of these words.

I did a study of three words: *marvelous, awesome,* and *wonderful.* In the New King James Version they are almost always used to describe God, His attributes, or His works. Think of it: *marvelous*—"full of marvel"; *awesome*—"full of awe"; *wonderful*—"full of wonder." Jesus is actually called Wonderful (Isa. 9:6). Yet today people use these words to describe common occurrences. They like a movie and they say, "It was marvelous," or "It was wonderful." They are impressed with an athlete and say, "He's awesome." Now when a preacher stands before people and says, "God is awesome," because they have heard that word repeatedly to describe an all-pro basketball player, they have no ability to understand the impact of what he is saying. I pray the message of this book will change that!

When Peter says that we have been called out of darkness into His marvelous light, he is using a very powerful word to communicate the greatness of God's nature. For God is absolute light, and in Him is no darkness at all. This great light speaks of His glory, which the human flesh is unable to approach.

Again, as with 2 Corinthians 6, we do not fully understand the impact of this statement because we do not understand its context. Let's return to Exodus to continue our quest of discovering the extent of God's promise to dwell among and in His people.

We Must Wash Our Clothes

In the last chapter we learned that Moses had led the children of Israel out of Egypt, which today is a type of our deliverance from the world. From Egypt he led them to the Mountain of God, called Sinai. He left them at the foot of the mountain and ascended to God, where he heard God say,

> "You have seen what I did to the Egyptians, and how I bore you on eagles' wings and brought you to Myself. Now therefore, if you will indeed obey My voice and keep My covenant, then you shall be a special treasure to Me above all people; for all the earth is Mine. And you shall be to Me a kingdom of priests and a holy nation." These are the words which you shall speak to the children of Israel. (Ex. 19:4–6 NKJV)

Now we know where Peter's words came from. They were originally spoken to the children of Israel. God did not speak these words just to Aaron and his sons. Nor did He speak them only to the tribe of Levi. He told the entire nation, every Hebrew man, woman, and child, "You shall be to Me a kingdom of priests." Do you see it was God's desire that they all enter His presence as Moses did?

> Then the LORD said to Moses, "Go to the people and consecrate them today and tomorrow, and let them wash their clothes. And let them be ready for the third day. For on the third day the

LORD will come down upon Mount Sinai in the sight of all the
people." (Ex. 19:10–11 NKJV)

We need to dissect carefully the meaning in these two verses. First
of all, this whole scenario is prophetic. Not only did it apply to
them, but it is also God's word to us. God told Moses that after two
days He was coming to the people. In that time period, Moses was
to consecrate them, which involved their washing their clothes.

We read in 2 Peter 3:8 (NKJV), "But, beloved, do not forget this
one thing, that with the Lord one day is as a thousand years, and a
thousand years as one day." And the psalmist wrote, "For a thousand years in Your sight are like yesterday when it is past" (Ps. 90:4
NKJV). One of God's days is a thousand of our years. So how long
has it been since Jesus has been raised from the dead? The answer
is, almost two days; we are at the very end of the second day.
Historians indicate that He was raised from the dead around A.D. 28
or 29. We are very close to His return, according to the prophetic
time clock! We immediately see the correlation between what God
said to Israel and what He is saying to us. Our responsibility as a
church has been to consecrate ourselves for the past two thousand
years in preparation for His coming!

What does *consecrate* mean? We rarely hear the term today.
Consecrate means "to sanctify," and *sanctify* means "to set apart." A
good example would be a woman selected to become the wife of a
king. She would be brought into the palace where the king's eunuchs
would care for her. The eunuchs' responsibility would be to prepare
her for the king. No longer would she live a normal life, as other
women would, for she was consecrated, sanctified, or set apart for
the king. However, if she cooperated, the sanctification would be a
small price compared to the tremendous benefits she would receive.
She would enjoy intimate privileges with the king no one else would
share. All that he had would be hers. In return, what did the king
expect from her? She was to be his, only his. This example perfectly

illustrates what God meant when He said, "You must be holy because I, the LORD, am holy. I have set you apart from all other people to be my very own" (Lev. 20:26 NLT).

God was saying to Israel when He told them to consecrate themselves, "I have delivered you out of Egypt. Now get Egypt out of you. This will prepare you for My coming on the beginning of the third day." He stated, "And let them wash their clothes." Their clothes still had the filth of Egypt on them.

Even so today God says to us, "I have delivered you out of the world, now get the world out of you! This will prepare you for My coming at the beginning of the third thousandth year." We are to rid ourselves of the filth of the world by washing our garments. Recall Paul's words: "Therefore, having these promises, beloved, let us cleanse ourselves from all filthiness of the flesh and spirit, perfecting holiness in the fear of God" (2 Cor. 7:1 NKJV).

Paul tells us to cleanse the garments of our flesh and spirits, even as Moses told the children of Israel to wash their physical clothes. I want to make a very pointed statement here: we are to wash ourselves. We are not to leave it to the Lord! Paul does not say, "And the blood of Jesus will rid you of all filthiness of the flesh and spirit, so just believe in His love." Does the blood of Jesus cleanse us from all sin or filthiness? The answer is undoubtedly yes! Yet, as we will see in Scripture, we have a part in this cleansing process.

TWO ERRONEOUS EXTREMES

For the last one hundred years there have been two extremes in the church in regard to sanctification and holiness. The first emphasized holiness as a completely outward condition. If a woman had on makeup, she was not holy. If she wore her dress above the knee, she was not pure. Well, a woman can have a dress down to her ankles and her hair up in a bun, with no makeup or jewelry on, and still have a seducing spirit up to her eyeballs! A man can boast about how he has never committed adultery or divorced his wife, but he may still lust after every woman who walks by him. That is not holiness. That extreme focused exclusively on the flesh, and holiness is not a work of the flesh. This notion led many people in the church into legalism.

The second extreme, which has become more prominent in the latter part of the century, is the belief that we do not have a responsibility to separate ourselves from the world. Christians are no different from the world except for the fact that we have been forgiven. Recently, a very popular Christian artist commented, "Christians go to counselors, Christians have family problems, and Christians become alcoholics. The only difference between believers and nonbelievers is our simple faith in our Creator God, who loves us and helps us every day." This kind of thinking has stemmed from our teachings that have absolved us of the responsibility of cleansing ourselves from the world. Yet this goes directly against what the Scriptures teach. Peter urges, "But now you must be holy in everything you do, just as God—who chose you to be his children—is holy" (1 Peter 1:15 NLT).

The truth lies in the middle of these two extremes. There is a cooperation between humanity and Deity when it comes to holiness. Jesus is our sanctification (1 Cor. 1:30). Yet "It is God's will that you should be sanctified: that you should avoid sexual immorality; that each of you should learn to control his own body in a way that is holy and honorable . . . For God did not call us to be impure, but to live a holy life" (1 Thess. 4:3–7 NIV). Jesus supplies the grace for our sanctification, but we must cooperate by cleansing ourselves through the power of that grace. In this way we are able to be in the world but not of it.

THAT WE MAY LIVE IN HIS SIGHT

God told Moses to sanctify the people. They were to prepare themselves because on the third day, the Lord would come down upon Mount Sinai in the sight of all the people! For God to come in the sight of all the people was for Him to come in His glory! The prophet Hosea also gives us a timetable of two thousand years to prepare for His coming glory. He cried out:

> Come, and let us return to the LORD;
> For He has torn, but He will heal us;
> He has stricken, but He will bind us up.
> After two days He will revive us;
> On the third day He will raise us up,
> That we may live in His sight. (Hos. 6:1–2 NKJV)

After two days, two thousand years, He will revive us, and on the third thousandth year He will raise us up that we may live in His sight. That third thousandth year is the millennial reign of Christ (this is when Christ will come to earth and reign a thousand years in His glorified body [Rev. 20:4]). Hosea goes on to say of His coming:

> Let us know,
> Let us pursue the knowledge of the LORD.
> His going forth is established as the morning. (Hos. 6:3 NKJV)

His going forth is established as the morning. The morning, or sunrise, comes at an appointed time each day. There is nothing you can do to change that time—absolutely nothing! It is coming whether or not you are ready. Jesus' coming, in His glory, is established, and nothing will change that appointed time. The question is, Will we be ready? The children of Israel believed they were, but were they? They had never seen His glory before. They saw His great signs and wonders and loved their benefit, but would His glory be the same? Can you be comfortable in the atmosphere of miracles, yet still be unprepared for His glory? Let's proceed to find out.

CHAPTER 4

THE GLORY OF THE LORD

The glory of the Lord is everything that makes God, God. All His characteristics, authority, power, and wisdom—literally, the immeasurable weight and magnitude of God.

Two days stood between the people of Israel and the glory of God. Were they ready? Did they take God's warning of preparation seriously, or did they reason that since they had seen His miracle power deliver them time and time again, His appearing would be no different? What more could it be? And besides, all the manifestations had been favorable to them. Why would His appearing be any different? Time would tell. Did any besides Moses think that possibly they had become too confident or familiar with the Holy One?

Two days passed. Morning was about to break forth on that third day. The atmosphere seemed unusually quiet. The eerie stillness before the invasion of the Almighty was almost unnerving. The people grew more and more uncertain. Creation was more aware of the One who was about to enter the surroundings than God's own people were.

The light of dawn was breaking forth, but it wasn't to be a typical sunrise. Suddenly, a dark cloud descended out of nowhere. The sight of it alone was terrifying enough, yet preceding its appearance was a very loud sounding of a trumpet. Louder and louder it blew! What could make such an intense sound?

As the cloud descended on the mountain, out of it came brilliant flashes of light and roaring thunders. The constant thunderings were different from anything the people had ever heard. They were accompanied by lightning flashes so bright that the sun seemed to darken from their intensity. The children of Israel shook with fear: "Moses himself was so frightened at the sight that he said, 'I am terrified and trembling'" (Heb. 12:21 NLT).

Despite his fear, Moses assumed his leadership role:

> Moses led them out from the camp to meet with God, and they stood at the foot of the mountain. All Mount Sinai was covered with smoke because the LORD had descended on it in the form of fire. The smoke billowed into the sky like smoke from a furnace, and the whole mountain shook with a violent earthquake. As the horn blast grew louder and louder, Moses spoke, and God thundered his reply for all to hear. (Ex. 19:17–19 NLT)

CREATION REVEALS HIS GREATNESS

The One who came down on that mountain was the One who designed and created the universe. The One who put the stars in their places with His fingers. The One who through knowledge and wisdom laid the foundations of the earth. The One who is from everlasting to everlasting!

For several years I have been concerned that we have lost sight of the awesomeness of the One we serve. Isaiah speaks often about God's greatness and majesty. The prophet questions,

> Do you not know?
> Have you not heard?
> Has it not been told you from the beginning?

He is baffled about why Israel has lost sight of the wonder of God. He declares:

> He sits enthroned above the circle of the earth,
>> and its people are like grasshoppers.
> He stretches out the heavens like a canopy,
>> and spreads them out like a tent to live in . . .
> "To whom will you compare me?
>> Or who is my equal?" says the Holy One.
> Lift your eyes and look to the heavens:
>> Who created all these?
> He who brings out the starry host one by one,
>> and calls them each by name.
> Because of his great power and mighty strength,
>> not one of them is missing. (Isa. 40:21–26 NIV)

God created the heavens with His hands by stretching out the universe like a canopy. And He was able to measure the universe with the span of His hand (Isa. 40:12)! Think of it—from His thumb to His pinkie, He measured the width, length, and depth of the universe!

Have you ever pondered the size of the universe? It is beyond your mental capacities. Maybe if we attempt to catch a glimpse of the vastness of the universe, we'll come closer to a peek at His glory. Scientists estimate that there are billions of galaxies in the universe, with each containing billions of stars. The sizes of these galaxies are quite small compared to the space that exists between them.

Our sun is located in one of these galaxies. When you look out into the sky at night, you are not seeing a picture of the entire universe—just the wee galaxy in which we live, called the Milky Way. And you see only a portion of it, for most of the stars in our tiny galaxy are too far away to be seen with the naked eye.

So let's begin with just the galaxy we live in. The closest star to our earth—other than our sun—is 4.3 light-years away. You may be thinking, *What is a light-year?* It is simply the distance light travels in one year. Light travels at the speed of 186,282 miles per second. That is roughly 670,000,000 miles per hour. Compare that to the speed of airplanes, which fly approximately 500 miles per hour. As you can see, light is very fast!

To give you an idea of how fast, let's assume you could fly a jumbo jet to the sun. When I fly to Asia, which is on the other side of the earth from where I live, it takes me approximately twenty-three hours. If I took that same plane on a nonstop flight to our sun, it would take roughly twenty-one years! Think of how long ago twenty-one years was. Think of all that time. Now imagine spending it all on an airplane just to get to our own sun. For those who prefer driving, it would take about two hundred years, not including gas or rest stops. How long does it take for light to travel to the earth? The answer is a mere eight minutes and twenty seconds.

Let's leave the sun and consider the nearest star. We already know it is 4.3 light-years from the earth. If we built a scale model of the earth, sun, and nearest star, and made our earth the size of a peppercorn, the sun would be the size of an eight-inch-diameter ball. According to this size scale, the distance from the earth to the sun would be twenty-six yards. Yet a scale airplane would take more than twenty-one years to span that twenty-six-yard distance.

So if this is the earth's and sun's ratio, can you guess the distance from the nearest star to our peppercorn earth? Would you think a thousand yards, two thousand yards, or maybe a mile? Not even close. Our nearest star would be four thousand miles away from the peppercorn! That means if you put the peppercorn earth in Miami, Florida, the sun would be twenty-six yards away, and the nearest star on our scale model would be positioned past Seattle, Washington, and into the Pacific Ocean a thousand miles out to sea! To reach this closest star by airplane would take approximately fifty-one billion years, nonstop! Yet light from this star travels to earth in only 4.3 years!

Most of the stars you see at night with the naked eye are one hundred to one thousand light-years away. However, you can see a few stars with the naked eye that are as far as four thousand light-years away (remember, they are not even the farthest stars in our tiny galaxy). I won't attempt to calculate the amount of time it would take for a plane to reach one of these stars. But when you look at one of the stars that is four thousand light-years away, you actually see light that left that star about the time Abraham married Sarah, and has been traveling at a speed of 670,000,000 miles per hour, without slowing down or ceasing since, and is just now getting to the earth!

These are stars in our tiny galaxy of the Milky Way. We haven't ventured out to the other billions of galaxies. And don't forget that there is mostly vast space between the galaxies. For example, a very close neighboring galaxy is named Andromeda. Its distance from us is approximately 2.3 million light-years. Think of it. It takes light traveling at a speed of 670 million miles per hour more than two million years to get to our earth from that galaxy! And it is our closest neighboring galaxy. There are billions of other galaxies. Have we gone beyond our ability to comprehend yet?

Isaiah declares that God measured this vast universe from His thumb to His pinkie! Solomon asserts by the Spirit of God, "But will God indeed dwell on the earth? Behold, heaven and the heaven of heavens cannot contain You" (1 Kings 8:27 NKJV). Are you getting a glimpse of who came down on that mountain?

To Whom Will You Compare Me?

Maybe we should discuss other matters small to God. Isaiah states that He weighed the mountains in His own scales and put the hills in a balance. He measured all the water in the oceans, seas, lakes, rivers, and ponds in the palm of His hand. He is the One who commanded the seas not to pass their boundaries (Isa. 40:12).

Have you considered the power of the seas? If a meteor one mile wide hit the Pacific Ocean a few hundred miles off Los Angeles, California, it would create a wave large enough to kill every person and wipe out every structure on the entire West Coast of America from San Diego to Anchorage, Alaska! It would continue across the ocean and wipe out several Asian countries as well. Yet the wave would not be nearly as tall as the Pacific Ocean is deep. So what would happen if the entire weight of the ocean waters was unleashed against mankind? There is a lot of power in the oceans of the world, yet God weighed every drop of that water in the palm of His hand!

THE LITTLE THINGS ARE A MARVEL

He has done astonishing works of great size and proportion, and His details are equally amazing. Scientists have spent years and expended vast amounts of money to study the workings of this natural world. They still have a small portion of the wisdom that went into His creation of this natural world. Many questions remain unanswered, however.

All forms of created life are based on cells. Cells are the building blocks of the human body, plants, animals, and every other living thing. The human body, which in itself is an engineering wonder, contains about 100,000,000,000,000 cells—can you comprehend that number?—of which there are a vast variety. In His wisdom, He designated these cells to perform specific tasks. They grow, multiply, and eventually die—right on schedule.

Though invisible to the naked eye, cells are not the smallest particles known to man. Cells consist of numerous tinier structures called molecules, which are comprised of even smaller structures called elements—and within elements can be found even tinier structures called atoms.

Atoms are so small that the period at the end of this sentence contains more than a billion of them. Yet an atom is made up almost entirely of empty space. The rest of the atom is composed of protons, neutrons, and electrons. Protons and neutrons are clustered together in a minuscule and extremely dense nucleus at the very center of the atom. Little bundles of energy called electrons whiz around this nucleus at the speed of light. These core building blocks hold all things together.

So where does the atom get its energy? And what force holds its energetic particles together? Scientists call it atomic energy. This scientific term describes what they cannot explain. God says He is "upholding all things by the word of His power" (Heb. 1:3 NKJV). And we read that "in him all things hold together" (Col. 1:17 NIV).

Stop and ponder this thought for just a moment. We have a glorious Maker whom even the universe cannot contain. He measures the universe by the span of His hand, yet He is so detailed in His design of the tiny earth and His creatures that modern science is baffled by it after years of study.

Of course, many books can be written about the wonders and wisdom of His creation. That is not my intent here. My purpose is to awaken amazement and wonder at the works of His hands, for they declare His great glory!

"WHO IS THIS THAT QUESTIONS MY WISDOM?"

Now you can better understand how Job felt after uttering foolish questions and statements in the ears of God and God came to him in a whirlwind and said,

> Who is this that questions my wisdom with such ignorant words? Brace yourself, because I have some questions for you, and you must answer them.

Where were you when I laid the foundations of the earth? Tell me, if you know so much. Do you know how its dimensions were determined and who did the surveying? What supports its foundations, and who laid its cornerstone? . . .

Who defined the boundaries of the sea as it burst from the womb, and as I clothed it with clouds and thick darkness? For I locked it behind barred gates, limiting its shores. I said, "Thus far and no farther will you come. Here your proud waves must stop!"

Have you ever commanded the morning to appear and caused the dawn to rise in the east? Have you ever told the daylight to spread to the ends of the earth, to bring an end to the night's wickedness? . . .

Do you know where the gates of death are located? Have you seen the gates of utter gloom? Do you realize the extent of the earth? Tell me about it if you know!

Where does the light come from, and where does the darkness go? Can you take it to its home? Do you know how to get there? . . .

Have you visited the treasuries of the snow? Have you seen where the hail is made and stored? I have reserved it for the time of trouble, for the day of battle and war. Where is the path to the origin of light? Where is the home of the east wind?

Who created a channel for the torrents of rain? Who laid out the path for the lightning? Who makes the rain fall on barren land, in a desert where no one lives? . . .

Can you hold back the movements of the stars? Are you able to restrain the Pleiades or Orion? Can you ensure the proper sequence of the seasons or guide the constellation of the Bear with her cubs across the heavens? Do you know the laws of the universe and how God rules the earth?

Can you shout to the clouds and make it rain? Can you make lightning appear and cause it to strike as you direct it? (Job 38:2–35 NLT)

When God finished speaking, an overwhelmed Job cried out,

> I have heard of You by the hearing of the ear,
> But now my eye sees You.
> Therefore I abhor myself,
> And repent in dust and ashes. (Job 42:5–6 NKJV)

Before Job's trials, God said that no one was like him on the entire planet. The Lord declared that he was a blameless and upright man, one who feared God and shunned evil. Job had not only heard the words of God, but had also taught his family and friends about them. Yet when he saw God, he cried out for mercy, for next to a holy God he was at best an undone man.

Isaiah was a faithful and godly man, but when he saw the Lord in a vision, he cried, "Woe is me, for I am undone! Because I am a man of unclean lips" (Isa. 6:5 NKJV). God's glory reveals our utter need for His grace, for without it we are doomed forever. He is so much greater than we can imagine. He is so great that the angels who have been near His throne for ages upon ages still cry out in holy fear, "Holy, Holy, Holy!" This is the One who came down upon the mountain in His glory before all of Israel.

UNAPPROACHABLE LIGHT

Now let's focus on what the glory of the Lord is. Some in the church have described the glory of God as a mist, a cloud, or a similar manifestation, and believers may state, "Oh, the glory of God fell in that meeting." But this statement limits and darkens His counsel by words without knowledge (Job 38:2).

First, the glory of God is not a cloud. You may ask, "Then why is a cloud mentioned almost every time God's glory is manifested in Scriptures?" God must hide Himself in the cloud because He is too magnificent to behold. If the cloud did not screen out His countenance, all flesh around Him would be consumed and instantly die. When Moses requested to see God's glory, the Lord's reply was firm: "You cannot see My face; for no man shall see Me, and live" (Ex. 33:20 NKJV).

Mortal flesh cannot stand in the presence of the holy Lord in His glory. He is the consuming fire in whom there is no darkness (Heb. 12:29; 1 John 1:5). Paul writes of Jesus: "He who is the blessed and only Potentate, the King of kings and Lord of lords, who alone has immortality, dwelling in unapproachable light, whom no man has seen or can see" (1 Tim. 6:15–16 NKJV).

This light is unlike any that we have on this earth. A friend of mine pastors in Alabama. Several years ago he was in a church under construction. There was an accident, and some heavy construction material fell on him, breaking his skull, neck, and back. The paramedics pronounced him dead when they arrived, and then covered him up.

I was on the golf course with him a few years ago and asked him to tell me of his experience with Jesus. I ruined his game because he cried nonstop from the fourteenth hole to the eighteenth hole as he talked.

He said, "John, I saw a great light from a distance and I traveled rapidly toward it. The closer I came, the more intense the light became. The light was too bright and white to compare to anything I can describe. It was so brilliant, I could barely stand to look at Him. Because of its intensity I could not see the facial features of Jesus, but I knew it was Him.

"All I could see was brilliant, almost unapproachable light. What stood out above all else was His holiness. The fire seemed to reveal it. I was aware that each cell of my being was exposed to Him. I felt as if the light of His being was cleansing me. As the light cleansed me I began to see His features, the first being His eyes. Those eyes were strong and piercing, yet full of love."

Eventually Jesus showed him that his work was not finished on the earth and that he had to go back. He had already been pronounced dead and covered with a sheet by the paramedics. When he returned to his body and began to move underneath the sheet, he terrified all those who were in the area. Today, he is a man of strong and deep prayer and lives a very godly life.

Paul states that Jesus dwells in unapproachable light, whom no man had seen or can see. The psalmist declares that the Lord wears light as a garment (Ps. 104:2; my pastor friend could see the Lord because he was not in his physical body). Paul experienced a measure of this unapproachable light on the road to Damascus. He related it this way to King Agrippa: "At midday, O king, along the road I saw a light from heaven, brighter than the sun, shining around me" (Acts 26:13 NKJV).

Paul did not see Jesus' face; he saw only the light emanating from Him, which overwhelmed the bright Middle Eastern sun at noon. I lived in Florida for twelve years, and it is called the Sunshine State. I never had to wear my sunglasses there. However, when I traveled to the Middle East, I had to wear sunglasses. The sun is much brighter there because it is a dry, desert climate. The sun was not so bad at eight or nine in the morning, but from eleven to two o'clock, it was very bright. Yet Paul said the light from Jesus was brighter! We train our kids never to look at the sun because it is much too bright for our eyes to handle. But imagine trying to look at the midday sun just in your area. It is difficult to look at unless it is veiled with a cloud. The glory of the Lord exceeds this brilliance manyfold.

Both Joel and Isaiah emphasized that in the last days when the glory of the Lord will be revealed, the sun will be turned into darkness:

Behold, the day of the LORD comes . . .
The stars of heaven and their constellations
Will not give their light;

The sun will be darkened in its going forth,
And the moon will not cause its light to shine. (Isa. 13:9–10 NKJV)

When we walk out on a clear night, what do we see? Stars every-where. But when the sun comes up in the morning, what happens? No more stars! Do the stars run away until after the sun goes down and then suddenly run back out in the sky? No. The glory of the stars is one level, but the glory of the sun is a much greater level. When the sun comes out, because it is so much brighter than the stars, it darkens them. When Jesus returns, because His glory is so much greater than the sun, He will darken it so that it will not be able to be seen, even though it is still burning! Hallelujah!

The glory of the Lord will overcome all other light. He is the perfect and all-consuming light. That is why in His second coming the men of this earth shall

Go into the holes of the rocks,
And into the caves of the earth,
From the terror of the LORD
And the glory of His majesty. (Isa. 2:19 NKJV)

ALL THAT MAKES GOD, GOD

What is the glory of the Lord? To answer, let's go to Moses' request to see God's glory: "And [Moses] said, 'Please, show me Your glory'" (Ex. 33:18 NKJV).

The Hebrew word for "glory" is *kabowd*. It is defined by Strong's Bible dictionary as "the weight of something, but only figuratively in a good sense." Its definition also speaks of splendor, abundance, and honor. Moses was asking, "Show me Yourself in all Your splendor." Carefully read God's response, "I will make all My goodness pass before you, and I will proclaim the name of the LORD before you" (Ex. 33:19 NKJV).

After Moses requested all His glory, God referred to it as "all My goodness." The Hebrew word for "goodness" is *tuwb*. It means "good in the widest sense." In other words, nothing is withheld.

God added, "I will proclaim the name of the LORD before you." Before an earthly king enters the throne room, the herald announces his name. The trumpets blow, then he enters the throne room in all his splendor. The king's greatness is revealed, and in his court there is no mistake about who is the king. However, if this monarch were wearing ordinary clothes and walking on a city street of his nation, without any attendants, people might pass by him without realizing his identity. In essence, that was exactly what God did for Moses. He was saying, "I will proclaim My own name and pass by you in all My splendor."

The glory of the Lord is revealed in the face of Jesus Christ (2 Cor. 4:6). Many have claimed to have seen a vision of Jesus and looked upon His face. That is very possible, but not in His full glory. Paul writes, "For now we see through a glass, darkly; but then face to face" (1 Cor. 13:12 KJV). His glory is veiled by darkened glass, for no man can look upon His full glory and live.

The disciples looked at the face of Jesus after He rose from the dead, but He did not openly display His glory. Some people saw the Lord, even in the Old Testament, but He was not revealed in His glory. The Lord appeared to Abraham by the terebinth trees of Mamre, but not in His glory (Gen. 18:1–2). Jacob wrestled with God, but not in His glory (Gen. 32:24–30).

Joshua looked at the face of the Lord before invading Jericho (Josh. 5:13–15 NKJV). The Lord appeared to him as a Man of war. Joshua did not realize who He was for he asked, "Are You for us or for our adversaries?" The Lord answered that He was the Commander of the army of the Lord and that Joshua was to take off his sandals because he stood on holy ground. Recall the example of the king not in his glory, dressed in ordinary clothes on a street of his kingdom.

People could pass by him without realizing his identity. That portrays what happened to Joshua.

The same is true after the Resurrection. Mary Magdalene was the first person to whom Jesus spoke, yet she thought He was the gardener (John 20:15–16). The disciples ate a fish breakfast with Jesus along the seashore (John 21:9–13). Two disciples walked with Jesus on the road to Emmaus, "but their eyes were restrained" (Luke 24:16 NKJV). All of them beheld His face because He did not openly display His glory.

In contrast, John the Apostle saw the Lord in the Spirit and had a totally different encounter from breakfast with Him by the sea, for John saw Him in His glory. He described Jesus as being:

> Like the Son of Man, clothed with a garment down to the feet and girded about the chest with a golden band. His head and hair were white like wool, as white as snow, and His eyes like a flame of fire; His feet were like fine brass, as if refined in a furnace, and His voice as the sound of many waters . . . and His countenance was like the sun shining in its strength. And when I saw Him, I fell at His feet as dead. (Rev. 1:13–17 NKJV)

His countenance is like the sun shining in its strength. How could John look at Him? He was in the Spirit.

The glory of the Lord is everything that makes God, God. All His characteristics, authority, power, and wisdom—literally, the immeasurable weight and magnitude of God. Nothing is hidden or held back! This is the One who came down on that mountain on the third day.

Was Israel prepared? How did the people respond to His glory? Will we be prepared at the end of the second thousandth year? How will we respond to His coming glory?

CHAPTER 5

THE PASS TO THE MOUNTAIN

God is calling us to His mountain to know Him intimately.
The pass to that mountain is holiness birthed out of
a heart that fears God.

$\mathbf{M}$any of the children of Israel probably thought they were ready for the third morning. They had seen God's delivering power work on their behalf time and time again. Yet they had not seen His revealed glory. Was their response what they thought it would be?

> Now all the people witnessed the thunderings, the lightning flashes, the sound of the trumpet, and the mountain smoking; and when the people saw it, they trembled and stood afar off. Then they said to Moses, "You speak with us, and we will hear; but let not God speak with us, lest we die." (Ex. 20:18–19 NKJV)

The people trembled and drew back. They did not want to hear God's audible voice, and they did not desire to stand in His glorious presence. The children of Israel had seen some of the greatest miracles that any generation has witnessed. How many preachers do you know that are splitting a lake, let alone an entire sea? How many ministers pray and enough bread falls from the sky each day to feed three million people? Experts estimate that each day enough manna fell to fill two freight trains, each having 110 boxcars!

Retreat from His Glory

The people were not so very different from our modern church. As for salvation, they came out of Egypt, which typifies the new birth experience. As for freedom, they experienced deliverance from their oppressors. In the same respect, "God has freed us from the power of darkness, and he brought us into the kingdom of his dear Son" (Col. 1:13 NCV). As for miracles, they experienced the benefits of the miracles of God, as have many in today's church.

What about prosperity? They experienced the wealth of the sinner that God had laid up for the just: "He also brought them out with silver and gold" (Ps. 105:37 NKJV).

What about healing? Scriptures record, "There was none feeble among His tribes" (Ps. 105:37 NKJV). Moses left Egypt with three million strong, healthy people. Can you imagine a city of three million with no one sick or in the hospital? The Israelites had suffered hardship for four hundred years. Imagine the healings and miracles that took place as they ate the Passover lamb!

The people were no strangers to God's saving, healing, miracle-working, and delivering power. They celebrated passionately whenever God moved miraculously on their behalf. They danced and praised God much as some do today in the church (Ex. 15:1, 20). So it is interesting to note that they were drawn to His miraculous manifestations because they benefited from them but were scared and drew back when His glory was revealed.

Why were the people so comfortable and even excited in the atmosphere of miracles, yet uncomfortable to the point of retreating in the presence of His glory? They could hide sin in the atmosphere of miracles.

A multitude will say to Jesus, "'Lord, Lord, have we not prophesied in Your name, cast out demons in Your name, and done many wonders in Your name?' And then I will declare to them, 'I never knew you; depart from Me, you who practice lawlessness!'" (Matt.

7:22–23 NKJV). The multitude was familiar with the signs and wonders of God and some even used to perform them, yet all the while they kept sin hidden in their lives. But no one can hide sin in the presence of His glory because His light exposes all things.

Jesus says to us in the new covenant,

> My friends, do not be afraid of those who kill the body, and after that have no more that they can do. But I will show you whom you should fear: Fear Him who, after He has killed, has power to cast into hell; yes, I say to you, fear Him! (Luke 12:4–5 NKJV)

Why does Jesus say this? The reason appears in the verses just before He exhorts us to fear God: "For there is nothing covered that will not be revealed, nor hidden that will not be known. Therefore whatever you have spoken in the dark will be heard in the light" (Luke 12:2–3 NKJV).

We can live with sin undetected around the miraculous, but sin cannot hide in the light of His revealed glory! Adam and Eve hid themselves from the glory of the Lord in the Garden after they disobeyed. There was a time when they walked with Him in the cool of the day (Gen. 2–3). Jesus explains, "They stay away from the light for fear their sins will be exposed" (John 3:20 NLT).

Moses urged the people: "Do not fear; for God has come to test you, and that His fear may be before you, so that you may not sin.' So the people stood afar off, but Moses drew near the thick darkness where God was" (Ex. 20:20–21 NKJV).

You might be thinking, *Moses drew near the thick darkness, not the light*. Remember, God is so brilliant that He had to hide in the thick dark cloud. Moses drew near the light of God, while the people drew away from it. Deuteronomy's account amplifies the people's response: "Surely the LORD our God has shown us His glory and His greatness, and we have heard His voice from the midst of the fire" (Deut. 5:24 NKJV). Can you imagine what it would have been like if the cloud wasn't thick and dark? His countenance is so awesome that they describe Him as a consuming fire, even though He was in a thick, dark cloud!

Moses was quick to warn the people, "Do not fear," encouraging them back into God's presence from which true life permeated. He told them that God had come to test them. Why does God test us? To see what is in us? No, He already knows. He tests us so that we might know what is in our hearts. The children of Israel needed to recognize whether or not they feared God. If they feared God, they would not sin. Sin results whenever we draw away from Him.

Moses said, "Do not fear," and then emphasized that God had come "that His fear may be before you." He clearly differentiated between being afraid of God and fearing God. Moses feared God, but the people loved themselves. To fear God is to love Him above all else! It is the willingness to obey God even when it appears more advantageous for you to compromise or not obey His Word. Those who love themselves cannot fear God. It is an infallible truth that if we do not fear God, we will be afraid of Him at the revelation of His glory and draw back. Remember that the people drew away from His glory but Moses drew near.

Deuteronomy's record of the incident was given years later to the younger generation before they entered the promised land. It reveals a point that Exodus does not show us. Moses reminded the people what happened when God's glory manifested in the dark cloud. They cried out to Moses: "You go near and hear all that the LORD our God may say, and tell us all that the LORD our God says to you, and we will hear and do it" (Deut. 5:27 NKJV).

They wanted Moses to hear for them, and they promised to listen to him and do whatever God said to do. They could keep in touch with God without having to deal with the darkness or sin hidden in their hearts. Good intentions do not always produce right results, for this nation of people tried this for fifteen hundred years and it did not give them the ability to walk in God's ways.

How many of us are like them? Do we get God's word from others but withdraw from the mountain of God? Are we afraid to hear His voice that lays bare the condition of our hearts? Are we concerned that if we draw too close, something may be revealed that we want to remain secret? If it is kept secret, we don't have to confront it, and we don't want to confront what we still enjoy.

THEIR DARKEST HOUR

Moses was disappointed with Israel's response. He couldn't understand their lack of hunger for God's presence. How could they be so foolish? How could they be so blind? Why would anyone refuse to have an audience with the living God?

Moses brought his deep concern before the Lord in hopes of a remedy. But hear what transpired between him and the Lord when he did: "Then the LORD heard the voice of your words when you spoke to me, and the LORD said to me: 'I have heard the voice of the words of this people which they have spoken to you. They are right in all that they have spoken'" (Deut. 5:28 NKJV).

Moses must have been surprised with God's answer. He more than likely thought, *What, they're right? For once these guys are actually right!* He must have cried out to God in his heart, "Why can't they come into Your presence as You have desired for them?" Before he was finished, God answered, and we can hear His sorrow in His words: "Oh, that they had such a heart in them that they would fear Me and always keep all My commandments, that it might be well with them and with their children forever!" (Deut. 5:29 NKJV).

The Lord wanted them to come to His holy mountain to behold Him. He wanted to reveal Himself to them, but they lacked what they needed to abide in His presence—holy fear. Now we can really hear His sorrow as He spoke to Moses: "Go and say to them, 'Return to your tents'" (Deut. 5:30 NKJV).

How utterly disappointing! It was their darkest hour. Many think their darkest hour came when they gave an evil report that kept them from the promised land or when they built the golden calf. No, my friend, this was their darkest hour. If they had sanctified their hearts, they would have been able to enter His glorious presence. Then the golden calf and the evil report that kept them from the promised land would never have happened.

This is true today. A man's darkest hour is not when he gets in bed with a woman who is not his wife or steals money from his employer. It happens when he refuses the invitation from the Lord to lay aside the desire of the world and come into the King's chamber for fellowship. Had he drawn near, the other never would have happened!

A young person's darkest hour does not happen when he gets drunk or stoned. It isn't when he is arrested for stealing. It happens when God calls him to draw near, but the popularity of his peers overrides the invitation of the King. Outwardly, it does not appear so dark, yet all of heaven grieves when God's call is taken for granted.

God told the children of Israel to go back to their tents, but He said to the man who feared Him: "But as for you, stand here by Me, and I will speak to you" (Deut. 5:31 NKJV).

Moses could stand near God and hear His words because of his fear of God. Any of the others could have been there, too, if they had cleansed themselves from the filth of Egypt in the fear of the Lord. Moses told them later: "The LORD talked with you face to face on the mountain from the midst of the fire. I stood between the LORD and you at that time, to declare to you the word of the LORD; for you were afraid because of the fire, and you did not go up the mountain" (Deut. 5:4–5 NKJV).

They believed they could not afford to have their hearts exposed by the light of His glory, so they retreated to a place where they felt safe. God's light would have only healed what it revealed, had they had the hearts to draw near, but they loved their state and did not desire to change.

Let's step back and look at the overall picture from God's perspective. God went to great lengths to bring His people out of bondage with signs, wonders, and miracles. The Scripture reports that He did it with a strong hand and an outstretched arm. He carefully led them and prepared them for His ultimate purpose, to bring them to Himself. He said to every one of them that His desire was that they would be priests unto Him and that He would dwell among them and be their God and they would be His people. What a love affair He planned for them! Yet when He brought them to Himself, they all ran away!

When did He become Father? Was it when Jesus was born? No! He has always had a Father's heart. Can you imagine how His heart felt when He carefully brought the people to Himself to reveal Himself to them and they ran away? It was heartbreaking!

A GLIMPSE OF GLORY

Now that we have seen from the report in Deuteronomy why the people withdrew, let's backtrack to the scene when God came down on the mountain. Once the people had withdrawn, God determined to start a priesthood. He would select a man who could come into His glorious presence for the people. He chose Aaron to be that priest. Once He had chosen Aaron: "Then the LORD said to [Moses], 'Away! Get down and then come up, you and Aaron with you'" (Ex. 19:24 NKJV).

However, Aaron did not end up near God's presence. He instead ended up with the people, withdrawing (Ex. 20:21).

God came again to Moses and said, "Come up to the LORD, you and Aaron, Nadab and Abihu, and seventy of the elders of Israel, and worship from afar. And Moses alone shall come near the LORD, but they shall not come near; nor shall the people go up with him" (Ex. 24:1–2 NKJV).

God asked for Aaron, his sons, and the elders of Israel, one of whom was Joshua. God did not ask Aaron to come up to the summit; he was to go to a place on the mountain above the camp. He had already withdrawn once because he did not fear God; he was able to worship only from afar. Many today worship the Lord from afar because it is safe. They avoid sanctifying their hearts, but they satisfy their inward need to worship the Lord.

In the men's worship they saw the God of Israel: "And there was under His feet as it were a paved work of sapphire stone, and it was like the very heavens in its clarity" (Ex. 24:10 NKJV). Matthew Henry's commentary states what I truly believe happened:

> They saw the God of Israel (v. 10), that is, they had some glimpse of his glory, in light and fire, though they saw no manner of similitude. They saw the place where the God of Israel stood (so the Septuagint), something that came near a similitude, but was not; whatever they saw, it was certainly something of which no image nor picture could be made, and yet enough to satisfy them that God was with them of a truth.

The men had a glimpse, but they were not permitted to enter His glorious presence. Moses' fear of God was the key to being asked to approach His presence. God invited him, "Come up to Me on the mountain and be there" (Ex. 24:12 NKJV).

Oh, how I love what God says to Moses. This is the secret place where God reveals His innermost thoughts and His ways. It is the place where His treasures are found. Isaiah announces to us,

> The LORD is exalted, for he dwells on high . . .
> He will be the sure foundation for your times,
> > a rich store of salvation and wisdom and knowledge;
> > the fear of the LORD is the key to this treasure.
> (Isa. 33:5–6 NIV)

A key unlocks the treasure of knowing God. We read that "he revealed his character to Moses and his deeds to the people of Israel"

(Ps. 103:7 NLT). Moses knew God's ways; he learned them on the mountain. The rest of the people could know God only by the miracles that He did in their lives. Oh, how many today know the Lord only by the miracles He has done in their lives? They may have experienced healed bodies, met needs, financial breakthroughs, or other answered petitions. These people have not gone to the mountain to learn His ways because they desire what this world can give them. They do not fear the Lord.

God is calling us to His mountain to know Him intimately. The pass to that mountain is holiness birthed out of a heart that fears God. He clearly tells us, "The secret of the LORD is with those who fear Him, and He will show them His covenant" (Ps. 25:14 NKJV).

CHAPTER 6

A MANAGEABLE DEITY

If you go to the mountain, you change. If you stay at the foot, as Aaron did, God's image in you changes.

What happens when people whom God has delivered from the world learn to live satisfied apart from His presence? In this chapter we discover the tragic result.

WAIT HERE UNTIL WE COME BACK

God sent the people back to their tents in the camp at the foot of the mountain. Moses, Aaron, and the seventy elders climbed up to a certain point to worship from afar. After a time of worship, God told only Moses to approach the top where He was. Moses chose Joshua to go up a little farther with him, but gave a concise directive to Aaron and the rest of the elders: "Wait here for us until we come back to you" (Ex. 24:14 NKJV). Then Moses went up to the summit of the mountain into the midst of the cloud and was there forty days and forty nights. Joshua waited somewhere between the location of the elders and the top where Moses was. And the people were in the camp, down below at the foot of the mountain.

As we saw earlier, Aaron was originally asked to come up with Moses. Why did he not go? He found more comfort in the presence of the people than in the presence of God. How do I know that? By his continual retreating from the glory of the Lord. The next time Aaron was mentioned, which was while Moses was on the mountain for that forty-day span, Aaron was back in the camp. And the other elders were with him!

The camp speaks of the familiar. It is the church that has been delivered from Egypt (the world) and is at the foot of God's mountain, but far enough from His presence to keep its heart from being exposed. I call it the familiar because it is not back in Egypt and it has all the forms of serving and moving with God, but in reality it is far from His heart. Aaron gravitated back there. How many do you want?

CHANGING THE IMAGE OF GOD

We can see in Aaron's life what happens when someone who has been delivered from the world by God's power chooses not to walk in His presence. Let's watch the tragic story unfold.

> Now when the people saw that Moses delayed coming down from the mountain, the people gathered together to Aaron, and said to him, "Come, make us gods that shall go before us; for as for this Moses, the man who brought us up out of the land of Egypt, we do not know what has become of him." (Ex. 32:1 NKJV)

Moses was on the mountain for some time. There was not any activity near the foot of the mountain, so the people did what religious people always do when God is not active: they gather together for a meeting. Though these meetings are done in the name of the Lord, they always produce what is very much against God's heart, as we will see.

The people gathered together to Aaron, the man who initially was supposed to go to the top with Moses, but didn't. He was to stay at a prescribed level and wait for Moses, but he didn't do that either. Why would the people gravitate toward such a man? Because he would give them what they wanted!

Aaron had a gift called leadership. Leadership is a gift from God (Rom. 12:8). It carries with it certain qualities, one of which is that it draws people like a magnet. And it will draw people, whether or not the man with it has been to the mountain! This explains how a man can have a church of five thousand people and God hasn't shown up! He uses his God-given gifts to carry out the people's desires, not God's. He has not been to the mountain to hear from God, yet he has a big following as a result of the gift! It's a sobering thought, isn't it?

The people urged Aaron, "Come, make us gods that shall go before us; for as for this Moses, the man who brought us up out of the land of Egypt, we do not know what has become of him." They did not say, "As for God, we do not know what has become of Him." They wanted to disqualify or discredit Moses.

In studying what the people said in the original language, I sometimes think the translators became a little nervous about the true meaning and used the English word *gods*. The Hebrew word for "gods" is *elohiym*. This word is found approximately 2,250 times in the Old Testament. Roughly 2,000 of its occurrences refer to almighty God, whom we serve. It occurs 32 times in Genesis 1. For example, the first verse reads: "In the beginning God [*elohiym*] created the heavens and the earth" (1:1 NKJV). Here *elohiym* is translated "God." And all the other times "God" appears in that chapter, it is the word *elohiym*.

Approximately 250 times in the Old Testament, *elohiym* is used to describe a false god. We always have to read it in context to understand the reference

Aaron said to the inquirers, "Break off the golden earrings which are in the ears of your wives, your sons, and your daughters, and bring them to me" (Ex. 32:2 NKJV). All the people broke off their earrings and took them to Aaron: "And he received the gold from their hand, and he fashioned it with an engraving tool, and made a molded calf" (Ex. 32:4 NKJV). In this verse, "fashioned" is the Hebrew word *yatsar*. It means "to mould into a form" (Strong's dictionary).

Once he formed this gold into a calf, all the people joined in, "This is your god, O Israel, that brought you out of the land of Egypt!" (Ex. 32:4 NKJV). The Hebrew word for "god" is again *elohiym*. You are probably starting to see what was happening.

"So when Aaron saw it, he built an altar before it. And Aaron made a proclamation and said, 'Tomorrow is a feast to the LORD'" (Ex. 32:5 NKJV). The Hebrew word for "LORD" here is *Jehovah* or *Yahweh*. *Yahweh*, the most sacred word in the Old Testament, is the proper name of the one, true God. It is never used to describe, or given as a name to, a false god. The word was so sacred that the Hebrew scribes wouldn't write it all out. They took out the vowels and wrote YHWH. It is referred to as the sacred tetragrammaton, the unspeakable four letters. It was the unmentionable name, the holy name guarded from profanity in the life of Israel.

In essence Aaron and the children of Israel made a molded calf, pointed to it, and said, "Behold Yahweh, the one, true God, who brought us out of the land of Egypt!" They did not say, "Behold Baal, the one who brought us out of Egypt." Nor did they ascribe their deliverance to any other false god. They called this calf the name of the Lord, reducing His glory to the level of the image of a golden calf. They acknowledged that Yahweh saved and delivered them from Egypt; they did not deny His healing power. They reduced His glory!

THIS CALF CAME OUT!

Meanwhile, Moses was with God on the mountain, and he was unaware of the people's activities. God commanded, "Go, get down!

For your people whom you brought out of the land of Egypt have corrupted themselves" (Ex. 32:7 NKJV). God's anger was very hot at that point. He called them "your people," not "My people."

God said they had "corrupted themselves." The word *corrupted* literally means "to decay." When we play church at the foot of God's mountain, we will eventually decay, for everything that is distanced from His heart will eventually deteriorate.

Later, God said of Israel,

> For My people have committed two evils:
> They have forsaken Me, the fountain of living waters,
> And hewn themselves cisterns—broken cisterns that
> can hold no water. (Jer. 2:13 NKJV)

He is the Fountain of Life. If we try to hold on to what He gave us in the past and play church at a place far from His heart, we will slide back. That is why Jesus stresses, "If anyone desires to come after Me, let him deny himself, and take up his cross daily, and follow Me" (Luke 9:23 NKJV). We must come to the mountain daily!

Moses came down from the mountain. When he entered the camp and saw the calf, his anger boiled. He questioned Aaron, "What did this people do to you that you have brought so great a sin upon them?"

Aaron defended himself, "Do not let the anger of my lord become hot. You know the people, that they are set on evil. For they said to me, 'Make us gods [*elohiym*] that shall go before us; as for this Moses, the man who brought us out of the land of Egypt, we do not know what has become of him.'" What he said was accurate, but he added, "I said to them, 'Whoever has any gold, let them break it off.' So they gave it to me, and I cast it into the fire, and this calf came out" (Ex. 32:21–24 NKJV).

"This calf came out." Can you believe he said that? We read earlier that he formed it with an engraving tool! He lied. It is one thing to lie when God is not angry, but to lie when He is already hot with anger is another thing.

I prayed about this: "Lord, not that I want to see this man judged or anything like that, but I don't understand. How did he get away with this bald-faced lie without the earth's opening up to swallow him? It appears You did nothing about his lie."

The Lord's response impacted my life in a great way and birthed the vision for this book. It opened up a whole new understanding of what has been going on in the church today. God said, "John, Aaron didn't go to the mountaintop. He didn't behold and abide with Me as Moses did. Therefore, his inward image of Me was shaped by the society in which he was raised. And that is what came out of him."

Aaron had spent all of his life up to that point, some eighty years, in Egypt. He was raised there; his parents were born and died there. He was surrounded by Egyptian culture, and Egypt had many objects of worship. Because Aaron did not go up to the mountain and commune with God and behold Him as Moses did, the image of Yahweh was forged by the society in which he was raised. Aaron glanced at the Lord from afar and saw God's feet. But he did not enter into His presence, as Moses did.

Jesus talks about "seeing" the kingdom and "entering" the kingdom (John 3:3, 5). We have to be born again, which is to be delivered from the world, to see the kingdom. But we are not to stop there; we are called to enter it. Paul said to men and women who were already saved in the cities of Lystra, Iconium, and Antioch, "We must through many tribulations enter the kingdom of God" (Acts 14:21–22 NKJV). God prepares already-saved people for what they will face to enter the kingdom.

Aaron was delivered from Egypt, which was a type of being born again, but he did not know God intimately. He played church at the foot of the mountain, which resulted in God's image being reduced to what he had absorbed from his surroundings.

A Different Jesus?

In the New Testament, Paul addresses this issue:

> For since the creation of the world His invisible attributes are clearly seen, being understood by the things that are made, even His eternal power and Godhead, so that they are without excuse, because, although they knew God, they did not glorify Him as God, nor were thankful. (Rom 1:20–21 NKJV)

They do not glorify Him as God. In other words, they know Him but give Him far less honor than He deserves. The children of Israel acknowledged the deliverance of Yahweh, but they did not give Him the honor, reverence, or glory of which He is worthy. Well, things don't change much. Paul goes on to say about people living in New Testament times:

> And changed the glory of the incorruptible God into an image made like corruptible man—and birds and four-footed animals and creeping things. (Rom. 1:23 NKJV)

The one, true God's glorious image is reduced to images of insects, birds, animals, and mortal man. Does our Western society worship birds, four-footed animals, or creeping things? Absolutely not. If we created an image of a calf from gold and put it on our front lawns, people would laugh at us and say, "Melt it down and make some jewelry out of it and sell it!"

What does our society worship? The answer is self, which is corruptible man! Israel was surrounded by a society that worshiped golden images of animals and insects. The modern-day church is surrounded by a culture that worships self or corruptible man. When Aaron and the people drew back from God's glorious presence on the mountain, their image of God was formed by what Egypt worshiped—

the images of animals. Today, when believers draw back from the mountain of God, their image of God is formed by what our society worships—self or corruptible man.

A thought has been running through my spirit for several years that I just cannot shake. That is, we have served a Jesus in the image we have made. We call Him Lord; we acknowledge His saving, healing, and delivering power. But is He the One sitting on the right hand of Majesty on high, or is He a Jesus that we have made more in the image of ourselves and still call Lord?

A MANAGEABLE DEITY

Idolatry is a very convenient form of worship. An idol gives its creators what they want—the dictates of their own hearts, since they are the ones who create it. Yet it satisfies the inborn need to worship a higher being. If the creators of the idol are passionate for sexual pleasures, then their idol will dictate to them ordinances that will gratify those desires. The Lord makes this very clear when He says through Isaiah: "Who would form a god or mold an image that profits him nothing?" (Isa. 44:10 NKJV).

Let's consider this motive in terms of what Israel did by returning to the point where Aaron created the calf of gold. He and the people regarded the golden calf as the image of Yahweh, who delivered them out of Egypt. "Then they rose early on the next day, offered burnt offerings, and brought peace offerings; and the people sat down to eat and drink, and rose up to play" (Ex. 32:6 NKJV).

The next day they went to their church service at the foot of God's mountain. They professed Yahweh's love and greatness. They gave their offerings, sang their songs, and preached their sermons. Their Yahweh gave them a message that they loved hearing since it gratified their desires. They sat down to eat and drink, then rose up to play. Their play was the pleasing of their own flesh. By the time Moses got to them, they were unrestrained (Ex. 32:25).

This scenario gives us greater insight into the root of idolatry. It is rebellion, and the Word of God affirms this: "Insubordination is as iniquity and idolatry" (1 Sam. 15:23 NASB).

All that the Egyptians had to do was to build a calf and call it some name, and it would give them what they knew in their hearts was against the Creator's wishes. (All men know His wishes, for Paul says, "God shows his anger from heaven against all sinful, wicked people who push the truth away from themselves. For the truth about God is known to them instinctively. God has put this knowledge in their hearts" [Rom. 1:18–19 NLT].)

For the Israelite who came out of Egypt, the basic concept is the same, but we must make one slight modification. The Israelite knew Yahweh's name and had already been touched by His power. If he did not want to give up his rebellious ways to conform to the ways of the Lord, then a way to satisfy both his conscience and his appetites was to create an image representing Yahweh that would give him what he desired. It was done ever so subtly, without his being consciously aware of it.

Paul warned the church at Corinth:

> I am afraid that just as Eve was deceived by the serpent's cunning, your minds may somehow be led astray from your sincere and pure devotion to Christ. For if someone comes to you and preaches a Jesus other than the Jesus we preached, or if you receive a different spirit from the one you received, or a different gospel from the one you accepted, you put up with it easily enough. (2 Cor. 11:3–4 NIV)

I like the Contemporary English Version's interpretation of verse 4: "We told you about Jesus, and you received the Holy Spirit and accepted our message. But you let some people tell you about another Jesus. Now you are ready to receive another spirit and accept a different message."

If we still desire a worldly lifestyle, which is against the flow of

God's authority, we can have it by subconsciously serving "our Jesus," whose will is in accordance with our own desires. Without realizing it we have a manageable deity! It is a subtle deception, not a blatant lie.

In our deception we comfort ourselves by saying, "Jesus is my friend," or "God knows my heart." It is true that God understands our hearts even more thoroughly than we can understand ourselves. But usually we make this comment in justification of actions that contradict His covenant. The fact is, it's rebellion. Our lips still honor Him, but our fear toward Him is taught by the precepts of men: "Wherefore the Lord said, Forasmuch as this people draw near me with their mouth, and with their lips do honor me, but have removed their heart far from me, and their fear toward me is taught by the precept of men" (Isa. 29:13 KJV).

We filter God's Word and commands through our culturally influenced thinking. Our image of His glory is formed by our limited perceptions rather than by His true image as revealed through His living Word on the mountain.

A SHARP CONTRAST BETWEEN TWO IN THE CHURCH

Allow me to give you a couple of examples. A woman called me and confessed that she had been in a physical adulterous relationship with a man in her church. Her husband was not a Christian and was verbally (not physically) abusive to her about her faith. In other words, he persecuted her.

She and the other man discontinued their physical relationship. Her "Christian friends" counseled her to divorce her husband and marry this nice Christian man who loved her because God had called her to peace. My question is, What "Jesus" do these friends of hers serve? Certainly not the One sitting on the right hand of God. Their image of Him has been shaped by society, for society is steeped in divorce. Most who have been divorced did not plan it.

They want a happy life based on their selfish interests. The covenant they made with their mates is significant only when it does not interfere with their happiness.

The woman asked for my opinion of her situation. She was really seeking permission from a leader to finalize the decision she was already embracing. Her husband had not been unfaithful morally; I told her that God hates divorce because it tears people's spirits and covers them with violence (Mal. 2:16). According to the New Testament, the Lord commands a wife not to depart from her husband, and if she does, she is not to marry again (1 Cor. 7:10–11). The woman mentally listened to me, but later I received the news that she divorced her husband and married the other man. She may be happy, but so were the people at the foot of the mountain until Moses came down!

On the other hand, I have known many God-fearing women who stayed in marriages with unbelieving husbands because they had the heart of God. They weren't seeking pleasure; they were seeking to serve. Many of the husbands eventually were saved because of the godly wives' lifestyles. Some, I might add, were saved after years of the wives' praying and living their testimonies before their husbands.

A different situation involved another woman who radiates the character of God. After being married several years, she discovered that her husband was a homosexual. For ten years she lived an unspeakably difficult life. He was arrested once for soliciting sex with an undercover policeman, and their oldest son received the phone call that his father was in jail.

The woman prayed constantly for her husband. When the going seemed too tough, she asked the Lord whether she should divorce him. The Lord replied, "You have scriptural grounds to divorce him, and if you choose to do it, I will bless you. But if you will stay and fight in prayer for him, I will bring him out and you will be doubly blessed." (Not that God would always say this in a morally unfaithful situation.) She chose to stay and fight, and it took some time. Her husband was gloriously set free and has been free for fifteen years. He is now a very compassionate senior pastor. I have preached for them, and I must say, she is one of the most godly women I have ever met.

Which woman has gone to the mountain to be transformed? The one divorced her husband out of a belief that Jesus wanted her to have peace, yet the Word of God clearly showed God's will for her was to stay with him. The other actually had scriptural grounds to divorce, but she chose to lay down her own rights to fight for the life of her husband. Jesus laid down His rights to come to this earth and die for us! Which woman had more of the heartbeat of God? Why? She has been to the mountain!

One of two things is going to happen in the life of a believer: either he is going to be conformed into the image of Jesus by allowing the Word of God that is spoken in the presence of the Lord to change him, or he is going to conform Jesus into the image of what his heart dictates. If you go to the mountain, you change. If you stay at the foot, as Aaron did, God's image in you changes.

When Moses came down from the mountain after forty days with God, he was changed, and his face shone: "When Moses came down from Mount Sinai with the two tablets of the Testimony in his hands, he was not aware that his face was radiant because he had spoken with the LORD" (Ex. 34:29 NIV).

The woman who stood for her husband is unaware of her purity. Every time I talk with her she reveals how God is dealing with her in regard to change. She does not realize how radiant she is. That is true for all who truly walk in holiness. As Scripture declares, "They looked to Him and were radiant" (Ps. 34:5 NKJV). Those who are able to look at Him are those who have removed the desires of Egypt from their hearts. They have one desire: to know the Lord of glory. So now we must confront ourselves with the important question, Is the Jesus we serve the One seated at the right hand of Majesty on high, or is He a different Jesus, who has been shaped by the ways and desires of the society we live in?

CHAPTER 7

INTENTIONS OR DESIRES?

We must bring our desires under the submission of the Cross.

All that we have discussed so far is a great introduction to the word *conform*. *Webster's Dictionary* defines it as "to reduce to a likeness in manners, opinions or moral qualities." The Word of God instructs, "Do not conform any longer to the pattern of this world, but be transformed by the renewing of your mind" (Rom. 12:2 NIV).

To better understand what the Spirit of God is communicating to us, let's go to the original. "Conform" in this verse is the Greek word *suschematizo*. The definition gives an even better picture of this word. Strong's dictionary defines it as "to fashion alike, i.e., conform to the same pattern (figuratively)." Vine's dictionary also defines it as "to fashion or shape one thing like another." Both dictionaries emphasize the thought of fashioning one thing into the likeness of another.

Aaron "fashioned" the gold that was given to him into the form of a calf. The outward act was only a reflection of what had been shaped within him. The influences of Egypt, from which he obviously did not cleanse himself, had been formed within his soul. What was in him was what came out. He had been conformed to Egypt, and, as we saw in the previous chapter, it was apparent that he did not desire to draw near to God's glorious presence to be transformed, as Moses did. And the people followed Aaron's example. God said about them:

> She [Israel] did not give up the prostitution she began in Egypt, when during her youth men slept with her, caressed her virgin bosom and poured out their lust upon her. (Ezek. 23:8 NIV)

According to the dictionary, the word *lust* simply means "desire." The Amplified Bible highlighted this meaning: "They poured out their sinful desire upon her." Desire is the motivating factor of human beings. We will always follow its course.

DESIRES AND INTENTIONS ARE NOT THE SAME

Desires and intentions are two different things, although many believe they are one and the same. You can have very good or godly intentions, but they may not be your true desires. Several people have told me that they desired to walk away from the influences of the world and press into God, yet they don't follow through. They are out of touch with their true desires, for James declares that "each one is tempted when he is drawn away by his own desires and enticed" (James 1:14 NKJV). Desire is the path that a person will take, no matter how good his intentions may be. For this reason, James goes on to say, "Do not be deceived, my beloved brethren" (James 1:16 NKJV). (Of course, there is a positive aspect of desire, but in this case we are dealing with the negative side.)

A comedian, not God, is the one who said, "The devil made me do it." The devil can't make a believer do anything. He can only entice, but you cannot be enticed with something you don't desire. If a line of cocaine or a few hits of LSD were offered to most believers, they would without hesitation refuse them, because they have no desire for them; therefore, they cannot be enticed by them. However, many believers, just as Israel, have not relinquished the desires that the world's system imparted to them as unbelievers. For this reason they can be easily enticed by those things.

We must bring our desires under submission of the Cross: "Those who are Christ's have crucified the flesh with its passions and desires" (Gal. 5:24 NKJV). It is not something God does for us; it is something we must do. We can't do it without His grace, yet we must do it! We can be enticed by any wrong desires that we have not put under the Cross. If we have not put away our desire for the world's ways, then we can easily slip back to the world, as Israel did. For this reason Paul confesses, "The world has been crucified to me, and I to the world" (Gal. 6:14 NKJV).

After I preached a message of repentance in a church in California, the pastor took me out to eat and shared a personal testimony. When he was saved, he gave up many former sins that bound him. However, he could not shake his habit of smoking two packs of cigarettes a day. He said, "John, I did everything scriptural that I knew to do to get rid of that addiction. I prayed, fasted, confessed the Word and asked others for prayer. In fact, I responded to the invitations to come for prayer of every visiting minister to our church. I confessed my addiction and asked them to pray for my deliverance. I did that for two years."

After two years of struggle, he took a friend to an evangelist's meeting at his church. The friend was not saved, and he, too, was addicted to cigarettes and smoked a couple of packs a day. That night his friend responded to the call of salvation, and when the evangelist prayed for him, he was gloriously saved and instantly delivered from cigarette addiction.

The pastor continued, "John, I was glad for my friend but very upset with God. I took my friend home and expressed my joy over his salvation the best I could. I went home and told God how upset I was. I sat in my living room and said, 'God, I have fasted, prayed, and humbled myself before my church and every minister who has come to our church, yet You have not delivered me. Tonight I bring

my friend, and instantly You save him and set him free from cigarettes. Why haven't You delivered me?'"

He then stated, "John, when I said that, God answered me in an
audible voice. Whether I heard Him with my ears inside or outside,
I don't know, but I do know that it was Him. When I cried out,
'God . . . why haven't You delivered me?' I heard Him firmly say,
'Because you still like them!'"

The pastor said, "I took one look at the cigarette that was in my
hand and I put it out, and I have never touched one since!"

Over that two-year span the pastor told himself and others how
he wanted to be free, yet it was not his true desire, only his intention. That is why he was so easily drawn to what he said he did not
want. Then God exposed his true desire. Once he repented of that
desire, placing it under the power of the Cross, the grace of God
was there to free him. His deliverance was a cooperation between
God and him.

This example directly applies to Israel and to the world's patterns,
ways, and mannerisms within the church today. Remember, Israel is
a type of the church. God said that Israel did not give up the prostitution she began in Egypt, when during her youth men slept with
her, caressed her virgin bosom, and poured out their desire upon
her. The people could have given it up, as Moses did, but they did
not want to.

THE DESIRE OF THE WORLD

Of all those who were delivered from Egypt, Moses was the one who
was most entangled in its ways. He was raised in Pharaoh's house, he
was schooled in Egyptian wisdom, and all of his friends were
Egyptian. The other Hebrew men and women were at least in their
own community within Egypt. They were treated harshly by that
society, yet Moses was treated well by its treasures and wisdom. They
had not been as involved with its whole system to the degree that

Moses had been. So if anyone could have said that he had it harder to get free from the desires of Egypt, it should have been Moses. Yet he had no desire for any form of Egypt, while the children of Israel continually gravitated toward it.

Today, we soften the message of the Cross for those who have come out of Hollywood, professional sports, public life, or some other walk of life greatly entangled with the world's system. We make concessions for them and excuse their worldly mannerisms or ways. We do this to their harm, not their good. When we preach a softer gospel to them, we block their way to the mountain of the Lord. They start out with excitement, yet gradually gravitate back to the world. If they do not go all the way back, they form a "Jesus" who is nothing like the One sitting on the right hand of God. They may confess salvation and a desire to know the Lord, but they are out of touch with their true desires. Their true desires are in the world's system. They are professing believers who are conformed to the world.

Israel confessed a desire to know God and to walk with Him. As you recall from previous chapters, before the Lord revealed His glory to the people on the mountain, He told Moses to inform the people that He had brought them to Himself. If they would obey His voice and keep His covenant, then they would be a kingdom of priests. Moses went down the mountain to report God's conditions to the people. Here is their response:

> So Moses came and called for the elders of the people, and laid before them all these words which the LORD commanded him. Then all the people answered together and said, "All that the LORD has spoken we will do." So Moses brought back the words of the people to the LORD. (Ex. 19:7–8 NKJV)

Their response was sincere, but we know what happened. They drew back, and the Lord's glory was altered within their hearts and minds. They spoke their intentions, not their desires. They were out of touch with their true desires, the desires of Egypt, which would keep them from drawing near to God.

A TYPE OF TWO GROUPS WITHIN THE CHURCH

Why did the people of Israel, who were less intertwined with Egypt's ways than Moses was, gravitate back to it, while Moses displayed no desire to have anything to do with its ways? Why was the one who was more entangled with the world less interested in its ways?

If we examine the two, we will find the difference. We will also have a very clear picture of two distinctive groups of people that make up the church today, with Moses representing one group and the children of Israel the other. We will see why many today in the church conform to the world while others in the church, even though some have come out of great entanglements of bondage, have no desire to return to the world.

For centuries the children of Israel had prayed and cried for deliverance from their Egyptian oppressors. They longed to return to the land of promise. God sent their deliverer, Moses. The Lord told Moses, "I have come down to deliver them out of the hand of the Egyptians, and to bring them up from that land to a good and large land, to a land flowing with milk and honey" (Ex. 3:8 NKJV). God then gave him His words and signs to command Pharaoh to let His people go.

Moses reentered Egypt for the first time in forty years to take God's word to Pharaoh. However, he first went to the people of Israel and told them God's message of freedom. When they heard the news, Scripture records: "So the people believed; and when they heard that the LORD had visited the children of Israel and that He had looked on their affliction, then they bowed their heads and worshiped" (Ex. 4:31 NKJV).

Can you imagine the feelings in that meeting? They had been slaves all their lives. Their fathers, grandfathers, and great-grandfathers had been slaves. The promise of deliverance and their own land had been talked about for four hundred years. (As a point of reference, the United States is less than two hundred and fifty years old.) And now they were looking at their deliverer.

The people experienced overwhelming joy. They saw the signs Moses performed and enthusiastically believed the report. I can just hear them crying, shouting and exclaiming, "What wonderful news! It has finally happened! God has come to set us free!" Their praise and thanksgiving eventually led them to bow their heads and worship God.

Moses left that meeting and went to Pharaoh and proclaimed the same message from the Lord. He commanded Pharaoh to "let His people go." But Pharaoh responded by increasing their hardship. No longer would straw be provided for the endless number of bricks that the Israelites were to produce each day. They would have to glean by night and labor by day. The total number of bricks would not diminish, although their straw was removed. God's word of freedom had increased their hardship and suffering.

The children of Israel's attitude started changing. They complained and told Moses, "Leave us alone and quit preaching to Pharaoh; you are making life worse for us." They were the same ones who had worshiped God just days earlier when Moses first brought the news.

When God finally delivered them from Egypt, Pharaoh's heart was hardened again, and he pursued the Israelites into the wilderness with his finest chariots and warriors. Seeing that Egypt had rallied against them and that they were backed up to the Red Sea, the Hebrews again complained: "Is this not the word that we told you in Egypt, saying, 'Let us alone that we may serve the Egyptians'? For it would have been better for us to serve the Egyptians than that we should die in the wilderness" (Ex. 14:12 NKJV).

"It would have been better for us."

In essence, they were saying, "Why should we do what you say God speaks when it is only making our lives more miserable? We are worse off—not better." They were quick to compare their former lifestyle with their present condition. Whenever the two did not balance, the Israelites wanted to go back. They desired whatever appeared to be their best interests over the desire to fulfill God's will. Oh, how they lacked true desire for God in their love for their own lives!

God split the sea, and the children of Israel crossed on dry land and saw their oppressors drowned. They believed and celebrated God's goodness with dancing and praising before Him: "Then Miriam the prophetess, Aaron's sister, took a tambourine in her hand, and all the women followed her, with tambourines and dancing" (Ex. 15:20 NIV). Can you imagine one million women dancing and playing tambourines? What a praise service!

They were firm believers, and nothing would draw them back. They were certain they would never again doubt His goodness! But they did not know their own hearts—their intentions, yes, but their desires, no. Another test would arise and again expose their unfaithfulness. Just three days later they complained that they wanted not bitter water, but sweet. (See Ex. 15:22–25.) Their thoughts were already turning to what they had in Egypt that they lacked in God's desert.

A few more days passed, and the children of Israel complained about the lack of food: "Oh, that we had died by the hand of the LORD in the land of Egypt" (Ex. 16:1–4 NKJV). They bring God into their complaints against His own will. How religious. Can you see their hypocrisy?

This same behavior continued until it climaxed when God took them to the wilderness of Paran. There the Lord instructed Moses to send twelve leaders from each tribe to investigate the land He had promised them. The leaders went to Canaan for forty days, and ten brought back a very discouraging report: "We are not able to go up against the people, for they are stronger than we" (Num. 13:31 NKJV).

Even though one leader, Caleb, strongly withstood the others (and Joshua joined him), the congregation embraced the bad report and wept and complained all night long: "Why has the

LORD brought us to this land to fall by the sword, that our wives and children should become victims? Would it not be better for us to return to Egypt?" (Num. 14:1–3 NKJV). They complained whenever they encountered situations that weren't to their liking. As long as it seemed good for them, they kept God's Word and appeared to desire Him. But if obedience meant to go a direction that wasn't pleasing to their flesh, the Israelites complained. "Would it not be better for us?"—these words paint a clear picture of their hearts. "For out of the abundance of the heart the mouth speaks" (Matt. 12:34 NKJV). Their core motivation for living was made evident by their behavior and words spoken under pressure; it was for themselves. Their focus was their own lives, not God's heart.

A DIFFERENT FOCUS

Moses was quite different. After becoming great in Egypt, he chose to suffer affliction with the people of God rather than enjoy the benefits of Egypt. The children of Israel did not choose their hardships, but Moses had been presented with the finest of everything the world could offer and refused it all: "He regarded disgrace for the sake of Christ as of greater value than the treasures of Egypt, because he was looking ahead to his reward" (Heb. 11:26 NIV).

Having quickly forgotten its oppression, the people of Israel wanted to return to Egypt (the world). They remembered only that they had feasted on the things they lacked in the wilderness of God's testing. Moses, on the other hand, chose hardship "because he was looking ahead to his reward."

What was that reward? The answer is found when God presented him with an offer that would have given him and the people the promise they had awaited more than four hundred years, the promised land. (This occurred before the leaders scouted out the land. The people were still looking anxiously for that land.)

75

The Lord said to Moses,

> Depart and go up from here, you and the people whom you have brought out of the land of Egypt, to the land of which I swore to Abraham, Isaac, and Jacob, saying, "To your descendants I will give it." And I will send My Angel before you, and I will drive out the Canaanite and the Amorite and the Hittite and the Perizzite and the Hivite and the Jebusite. (Ex. 33:1–2 NKJV)

The offer of the promise they had awaited was before them. After four hundred years in a foreign land, the offer of a bountiful land was being laid before the leader. But there was a catch. God continued, "Go up to a land flowing with milk and honey; for I will not go up in your midst, lest I consume you on the way, for you are a stiff-necked people" (Ex. 33:3 NKJV).

God told Moses to take the people to the land He had promised them, the very land they had waited hundreds of years to inherit. God even promised Moses the escort of a choice angel, although He would not accompany them.

Moses quickly responded, "If Your Presence does not go with us, do not bring us up from here" (Ex. 33:15 NKJV). Moses did not hesitate or bargain in his answer. He would without a second thought remain in the arid desert, the place that brought much discomfort with God's presence, rather than go to the land of vineyards, streams, and beautiful houses without God's presence.

I am glad that the option of entering the promised land without God was not placed before the children of Israel. They continually complained in difficult times with threats to return to Egypt, and if they would have taken Egypt without God, they would have gladly taken their own good land with an angel. Their reward was whatever benefited them the most. (This is what the world lives for, too—"What is best for me?")

To Moses, the promise was nothing without God's presence. He refused God's offer because even though it would have resulted in a much more comfortable life, it was void of what his heart beat for. He desired above all else to know God: "If you are pleased with me, teach me your ways so I may know you" (Ex. 33:13 NIV).

He did not ask for land, wealth, honor, or any other tangible asset. He had it all in Egypt and realized that it did not bring true satisfaction. Immediately after he refused the offer of the promised land void of God's presence, his heart cry was, "Please, show me Your glory" (Ex. 33:18 NKJV).

Moses made a firm decision. He pursued the reward of knowing God. Shunning the world was no price at all in comparison with the reward of God's glory. Because he decided to forsake the rewards of the world's system, he was able to draw near to God on the mountain. The people, however, couldn't draw near to the God of holiness. Egypt's desires were still within them. They had not separated themselves in their hearts from the world, which resulted in their inability to separate what was of the world and what was of God.

If you desire both the world and the intimate knowledge of God, the image of God becomes distorted. You do not truly know Him; you know a different Jesus. The children of Israel wanted God's deliverance, but desired what Egypt had as well. That was why they never would "give up the prostitution they began in Egypt." They were conformed to the world, Egypt's desires were shaped within them, and even though God's strong power delivered them out of Egypt, they did not make the decision to get Egypt out of them.

CORE MOTIVATION FOR LIFE

The separating factor between Moses and the people of Israel was their inward motivation for life. Moses wanted God and would gladly pay any price to know Him. The children of Israel wanted what was best for them. If the benefit of walking in God's way was evident to their natural senses, then they would gladly embrace it, but if it was not evident, they would gravitate toward what seemed best. To know God will always result in what is best for us, for God is perfect love. However, many times this knowledge will not be evident to the natural senses.

Moses loved God for who He was; Israel loved God for what He could do for them. If what He was doing did not meet their desires, they moved toward what they deemed best. Israel's view of life was little different from the core motivating factor of the world. John declared, "For all that is in the world—the lust [desire] of the flesh, the lust [desire] of the eyes, and the pride of life—is not of the Father but is of the world" (1 John 2:16 NKJV).

Those in the world desire what will please and gratify their senses or status. That was the way Israel lived, and if obedience to God showed immediate benefits, they would gladly follow.

Moses and Israel perfectly illustrate the two groups of people that make up the church today. This fundamental difference is the dividing line in the church, which reveals the genuine worshipers and those who profess Jesus as Lord, yet are self-seeking.

Now we can more clearly understand Jesus' words in the New Testament:

> When He had called the people to Himself, with His disciples also, He said to them, "Whoever desires to come after Me, let him deny himself, and take up his cross, and follow Me. For whoever desires to save his life will lose it, but whoever loses his life for My sake and the gospel's will save it." (Mark 8:34–35 NKJV)

The Cross represents complete death to our desires and wishes. Those who embrace the Cross trust that God is a faithful, just, and loving Creator and Master. They know that all life proceeds from Him, and outside Him there is no true life.

Moses saw the big picture; Israel could see only themselves. Moses understood that God is holy and to draw near to Him required the complete forsaking of the world and its very form. He realized that in denying himself, he would gain the knowledge of God. Paul saw the big picture as well, and we see his core motivation for life in these comments to two churches:

> As for me, God forbid that I should boast about anything except the cross of our Lord Jesus Christ. Because of that cross, my interest in this world died long ago, and the world's interest in me is also long dead. (Gal. 6:14 NLT)

> Whatever was to my profit I now consider loss for the sake of Christ. What is more, I consider everything a loss compared to the surpassing greatness of knowing Christ Jesus my Lord, for whose sake I have lost all things. I consider them rubbish, that I may gain Christ. (Phil. 3:7–8 NIV)

He was not deceived. He had no desire for the world. The price of forsaking its pleasures and benefits was no price at all compared to the unsurpassing greatness of knowing and walking with the One who is Life.

CHAPTER 8

COUNTERCULTURE OR SUBCULTURE?

*We are not to imitate the world's patterns or mannerisms
or to act like the people of this world.*

The people could not bear the manifestation of God upon His mountain. Before God's glory was revealed, the people professed their desire for Him, yet in actuality they did not. In their hearts they had not separated themselves from Egypt; they had not forsaken their desire for its ways. But when "God" was offered in a package similar to the mannerisms and patterns of Egypt, it was wonderful, they thought, because they could have God and their true desire—Egypt. They could remain conformed to Egypt and have Yahweh too!

Numerous patterns and mannerisms of lifestyles are shaped by the spirit of the world. (Satan is referred to as "the prince of the power of the air" [Eph. 2:2 NKJV] and "the god of this age" [2 Cor. 4:4 NKJV].) If we do not choose to forsake them, for the reward of drawing near God's presence, we will constantly gravitate back toward the influences of the spirit that runs the world. But God commands, "Do not act like the people in Egypt, where you used to live . . . You must not imitate their way of life" (Lev. 18:3 NLT).

We are not to imitate the world's patterns or mannerisms or to act like the people of this world. Paul reinforces this point: "Do not conform any longer to the pattern of this world, but be transformed by the renewing of your mind" (Rom. 12:2 NIV).

The kingdom of God and the course of this world are running in two opposite directions. There is no harmony between the two, as Jesus indicates, "When the world hates you, remember it hated me before it hated you. The world would love you if you belonged to it, but you don't. I chose you to come out of the world, and so it hates you" (John 15:18–19 NLT).

Jesus chose us to come out of the world's pattern of living, and He explains, that's why it hates us. But does it really hate us? It is almost as if the church has spent the past few decades trying to prove Jesus' words here to be inaccurate. We have tried our best to fit in. We have unconsciously believed we could have the world's approval and Jesus' approval too! But Jesus says that the world will love us only if we belong to it. So have we strived to belong where we shouldn't fit in?

THE EARLY CHURCH COMPARED TO TODAY'S CHURCH

I have done some reading about the early church, mostly the second- and third-century church, and I have discovered a huge difference between them and us. Their outstanding characteristic was their separated lifestyle. No one could find the mannerisms, methods, and ways of the world in them. They were completely different from their surrounding society because they lived under a totally different set of principles and values. The Word of God truly shaped their lives.

The reports of these early believers by the unbelievers were that Christians dwelt in their communities as sojourners, and that even though they lived in the flesh, they did not live after the flesh. They obeyed the prescribed laws, and at the same time, they surpassed the laws by their lives. They had little interest in respectable pleasures, public sporting events, and amusements. They loved all men but were persecuted by all. They were dishonored, but in their very dishonor were glorified. And those who hated them were unable to give any reason for their hatred.

Presently, those who hate us don't have to search too hard to give valid reasons for their dislike. This report given of the early Christians could apply only to a small segment of today's church. We have had numerous scandals at all levels of ministry. These tragic incidents have occurred because of our self-seeking desires. Not only leaders but many in the church live materialistic lives in the pursuit of pleasures and treasures of this world. We think nothing of lining up for the same movies, entertainment, and amusements that the world pursues.

Cyprian was a very wealthy Roman who gave his life to Jesus at the age of forty. He was so jubilant to have found Christ that he liquidated all of his assets and gave away his money to those in need. He later became an overseer in the church. He wrote,

> The one peaceful and trustworthy tranquility, the one security that is solid, firm, and never changing, is this: for a man to withdraw from the distractions of this world, anchor himself to the firm ground of salvation, and lift his eyes from earth to heaven (the mountain of God) . . .
>
> He who is actually greater than the world can crave nothing, can desire nothing, from this world. (Cyprian's Letter to Donatus, sec. 14)

The early Christians believed that this world and the next were two enemies; therefore, we cannot be the friends of both. James bluntly states, "You adulterers! Don't you realize that friendship with this world makes you an enemy of God? I say it again, that if your aim is to enjoy this world, you can't be a friend of God" (James 4:4 NLT).

Why does he call believers adulterers who seek to enjoy this world? An adulterer has a covenant with one but seeks a relationship with another. We as believers have a covenant with God, so why would we desire to pursue the patterns, mannerisms, and ways of the world? Could it be that we are no different from Israel of old, who would not give up the desires of Egypt for the privilege of coming to God?

COUNTERCULTURE VS. SUBCULTURE

The early church was a counterculture. Today much of the church is a subculture. What is the difference? A *counterculture* is a group of people whose lifestyle rejects or opposes the dominant values and behavioral patterns of society. A completely different set of guidelines governs their lives. The early church depicted this. Peter said to the first converts, "Be saved from this perverse generation" (Acts 2:40 NKJV). *The Message* heightens the meaning by quoting Peter as saying, "Get out while you can; get out of this sick and stupid culture!"

A *subculture*, on the other hand, is a distinctive group of people that is still part of the overall existing culture. Though some trait about people in the group distinguishes them, they are connected with society overall. The church today fits this description. We have our labels of "born again" and "saved." We affiliate with groups or circles: evangelical, Full Gospel, charismatic, denominational, and so on. But we are very much tied in with society.

Our society encompasses people with vastly different lifestyles. If we drew a graph sketching the lifestyles of Americans, we would have, on one end, extreme liberals and, on the other end, conservatives, with many variations between the two ends. On the extreme liberal end, we find people such as rock stars, celebrities, and others who dress up in unusual clothing, some even dressing in what the opposite sex usually wears. These people live an exceptionally abnormal life performing lewd acts both privately and publicly. Some die their hair black and bleach their skin. Others live perverted lifestyles.

We consider them an extreme segment of society that most of the church would never seek to emulate.

On the other end, we find the conservative Americans. These men and women live what many call normal lives. Although this segment of society sees itself as "good," it is linked with the overall culture living under the influence of the prince of the power of the air. Sometimes "good" is the greatest enemy of God. Remember, Eve's choice of what seemed good was very much against God's ways.

Instead of believers living totally separate lives today based on the governing authority of the kingdom of God, many of us live our lives no differently from conservative unbelievers. We say we are not of this world, but for many of us this is a theory instead of a reality. Because we are connected, as the boundary lines of society shift, we shift with them.

The Word of God instructs believers to "abstain from every form of evil" (1 Thess. 5:22 NKJV). And we are exhorted to "take no part in the worthless deeds of evil and darkness; instead, rebuke and expose them. It is shameful even to talk about the things that ungodly people do in secret" (Eph. 5:11–12 NLT). But have we heeded these warnings?

Today the movie industry places ratings on its movies. Most believers as well as conservative Americans think nothing of viewing a typical PG-13 movie as long as it does not have excessive profanity or nudity. However, many of these movies, while they don't have excessive profanity or nudity, are filled with disrespect, anger, hatred, violence, or implied extramarital affairs. Many believers will view such ungodly behavior without a second thought.

Yet let's take that same PG-13-rated movie and show it to the people of this country in the 1940s. What would have been their reaction? Most would have been horrified at the contents! What has happened? The lines of conservative America have shifted, and the church's lines have moved with them. What would have shocked unbelievers in America in the 1940s is considered normal by most believers in the church today. Have we been governed by the ways of the kingdom of God, or have we been influenced by the desires of Egypt?

The ways and standards of the kingdom of God are consistent, for God does not change. Scripture declares that there isn't a shadow of turning in Him. When God tells us to avoid even the form of evil, and says that it is shameful even to talk about the things that ungodly people do, why do we line up or subscribe and pay money to see attitudes, mannerisms, and patterns that have been shaped by the perverted generation we live in? A friend told me that while he was deep in prayer, he heard the Lord passionately question, "Why do My people entertain themselves with the very things that drove the nails through My hands?"

Does the entertainment industry have discernment? Do the executives and decision makers know the fruit that God seeks in His people? So why do we rely on the ratings of the industry instead of discernment? Has God changed in the past twenty years to accommodate the trends of this generation? Absolutely not! If God's standards have not changed, why have the average American believer's standards changed? We have been linked to the culture, not to the kingdom, in our lifestyles. We have not forsaken the desires of Egypt. This pattern is evident in all areas of life—clothing, hairstyles, ways in which we handle money and business, views of politics, and more.

The people in the early church were able to reject the ungodly attitudes, mannerisms, and entertainment of their culture because they conformed to the ways of the kingdom of God. They were a hungry church, and they desired to know their Redeemer more than they desired comfort or pleasure. The enticements of their culture had no power over the majority of them because of their passion for the Lord. The cost of forsaking all was nothing compared to the reward of knowing the Redeemer. They not only acknowledged it but lived it as well. This lifestyle produced a healthy discipline among them.

Unlike some denominations or groups that came later, the early believers generally didn't try to legislate holiness through excessive rules, laws, or regulations. They depended on sound doctrine, the genuine leading of the Spirit, godly example, and a firm commitment to serve. Churches that depend on external regulations to bring about holiness usually end up generating religious legalists. The early church stressed the importance of a changed heart, which would produce a godly lifestyle. Outward mannerisms were considered useless if they did not reveal what was happening within a person.

ARE WE AROUSING THE LORD'S JEALOUSY?

Today we have invited the world into our homes through television, videos, magazines, newspapers, and so forth. Many times I have grieved at the sight of posters of athletes, pictures of movie stars hanging on the children's walls, and magazines of Hollywood stars and other idols of society in the homes of believers. Why have we lifted up these men and women idolized by society?

In speaking of idols Paul warned, "You cannot drink the cup of the Lord and the cup of demons too; you cannot have a part in both the Lord's table and the table of demons." Why do we want to feed off of what the world feeds off of? He added, "Are we trying to arouse the Lord's jealousy?" (1 Cor. 10:21–22 NIV). Why are we so interested in what interests the world?

For years my family has been acquainted with a well-known professional wrestler. His family has been touched by God in many ways. The mother and children and a relative have been saved. The wrestler has also heard the gospel from us; he knows there is a price to pay to follow Jesus, and he is not yet willing to lay all down to follow Him. In one sense, I respect him for his honesty because many in the church say they will forsake all to follow Jesus, yet they do not follow through on their words.

I have used this wrestler as an allegory when speaking of spiritual strength in messages I've given in Christian conferences and churches around the country. My heart has almost broken when people come up to me with excitement and want to know who he is. I have wanted to cry out, "How should you know who he is? Why have you been watching professional wrestling?" At the risk of sounding legalistic I refrain. Perhaps I shouldn't. I care a great deal for him, but I cannot bear to watch him on television since the act is so full of darkness. I think, *How can believers watch this on a regular basis? Where is their zeal for God's presence?*

A WAKE-UP CALL

Some time ago I had a wake-up call that has fueled my passion for this message. I had ministered in a church on seeking God. The powerful service deeply moved many people.

The next day was a time of rest for me. I was traveling with my wife and children, and we had been on the road for some time. The pastor invited all of the leaders over for fellowship. We ate and talked, and much of the conversation concerned God's touch on them in the service the previous day. After supper we decided to watch a movie. Someone had a video of a movie that had been very popular. I thought the leading actor was gifted, and although it was rated PG-13, I spoke up, saying I wanted to see it.

At the very beginning there was a graphic murder scene. I was troubled by it but decided to continue to watch. Though the movie had no more killing, a lot of fighting, hatred, rage, bitterness, and deception occurred. As I watched I felt alarm in my heart. I kept thinking that we were earlier speaking about the things of God, sensing life and light, and now we were opening ourselves to darkness. I felt that I was being a terrible witness.

Then one of my sons stepped into the room at the moment the actor flashed back to the murder. My son was horrified. He ran out of the room and was so disturbed that he and his older brother went to my wife (who had left at the beginning) for comfort. He couldn't understand how his father could watch such a picture. He asked, "Mom, that movie is rated PG-13 or R. Why is Dad watching it?"

When the movie was over, I felt violated. I knew I had done something foolish. I said my good-byes to the leaders. It was the last time I saw them on that trip. What a way to leave them! I apologized to my wife, who told me about my son's comment. I apologized to the boys the next day and told them how wrong I was. I had sinned against God, them, and those leaders. They were very gracious and forgave me, but they were still working through it.

In another city we stayed with a godly couple who are very close to me. When I was first born again in the late seventies, they came into my life and mentored me. He was a researcher at Purdue University. He has led many to the Lord and has helped many students grow in the Lord. He loves to talk about the things of the kingdom.

My son told this couple of the movie his dad had watched at the pastor's home. My wife later told me what he had done. They were so pure, I was ashamed and deeply saddened that my old friends knew what I had done.

I immediately went to the Lord in prayer. God spoke to me in no uncertain terms and showed me it was a wake-up call. If I was so grieved by the couple hearing the news, how do I think He responded to my submitting myself as His temple to such darkness? I was overwhelmed with sorrow. Thank God, He is gracious and merciful in His forgiveness!

AN EYE-OPENING REVELATION

The Lord used this incident to show me His truth concerning our responsibility to separate from the world. His revelation, as it always does, reshaped my thinking and way of life. Later that week the Lord used the life of Lot, Abram's nephew, to further illustrate this truth.

God told Abram to leave his country, his relatives, and his father's house, and He would make Abram a great nation and bless him. Abram departed, and his nephew, Lot, went with him. The departure of the men was a type of being saved, just as with Moses and Israel coming out of Egypt. Abram left his home out of revelation, whereas Lot did not. Abram had the same motive as Moses, whereas Lot was more like the children of Israel.

The result of Lot's leaving with Abram was that he entered into the blessings of God. Abram prospered and was very rich in livestock, silver, and gold (Gen. 13:2). And Lot, "who was traveling with Abram, was also very wealthy with sheep, cattle, and many tents" (Gen. 13:5 NLT). However, whenever someone who is seeking his own benefit moves with someone who is seeking God, a conflict will result, because the flesh will always resist and eventually contend with the spirit. And so we learn that "there was strife between the herdsmen of Abram's livestock and the herdsmen of Lot's livestock" (Gen. 13:7 NKJV). Being the one after God's heart, Abram said to his nephew,

> Please let there be no strife between you and me, and between my herdsmen and your herdsmen; for we are brethren. Is not the whole land before you? Please separate from me. If you take the left, then I will go to the right; or, if you go to the right, then I will go to the left. (Gen. 13:8–9 NKJV)

Abram's heart was after God. His interests in personal gain were no longer the driving forces in his life. What the world could provide him no longer mattered because, "he was looking forward to the city with foundations, whose architect and builder is God" (Heb. 11:10 NIV). His eyes were set on the eternal; getting best choice of the land didn't matter to him.

Those who have been saved yet lack passion for God, as the children of Israel, will seek their best interest in this world's system, for that is where their reward lies. Abram yielded to Lot by giving him first choice of the land.

> Lot took a long look at the fertile plains of the Jordan Valley in the direction of Zoar. The whole area was well watered everywhere, like the garden of the LORD or the beautiful land of Egypt. (This was before the LORD had destroyed Sodom and Gomorrah.) Lot chose that land for himself—the Jordan Valley to the east of them. He went there with his flocks and servants and parted company with his uncle Abram. So while Abram stayed in the land of Canaan, Lot moved his tents to a place near Sodom. (Gen. 13:10–12 NLT)

The land Lot chose was very inviting. He could see prosperity and comfort awaiting him in those plains. He was familiar with the territory, for they had passed through the area before (Gen. 13:3). He probably knew that "the people of this area were unusually wicked and sinned greatly against the LORD" (Gen. 13:13 NLT). Perhaps that accounts for the "long look" he took. I imagine he was weighing the blessing of the land against the evil accompanying it. But the desire for "the good life" was stronger in him than the passion for God, which Abram possessed. Therefore, Lot overlooked the wickedness of the land. He more than likely thought that he could remain unaffected by it.

I believe he "moved his tents to a place near Sodom" to stay away from the hub of the wicked society. He behaved much like many believers today. They think, *I can get a little involved in the world's system, away from its wicked segments, without getting sucked into it.* These thoughts are at best foolish! The world has an attracting force within it called seduction, and if you have any desire for selfish gain, it will pull you in, just like a magnet will draw certain metals and not affect others at all.

Lot's intentions might have been good to stay away from the city of Sodom, but later he no longer lived in a tent near the city. He had moved into a house within the gates of the city of Sodom (Gen. 19:1–3)! He was drawn into it. I am sure that the benefits drew him in, yet we read in the New Testament that his righteous soul was vexed by the filthy conduct of the unrighteous: "For that righteous man [Lot], dwelling among them, tormented his righteous soul from day to day by seeing and hearing their lawless deeds" (2 Peter 2:8 NKJV).

I will never forget what God revealed to me that week. The words "seeing and hearing their lawless deeds" stood out to me. In seeing and hearing their lawless deeds, Lot vexed his righteous soul.

You may be thinking, *I see and hear lawless deeds every day. I see and hear them at work, in school, in public. How can I keep from vexing my soul?* The Lord showed me the key. When you go to work, school, or any other place to carry out necessary daily activities, you are going into your mission field. God is sending you out to be a light in dark places. You will reach people there with your witness of Jesus' resurrection power that might otherwise never step foot into a gospel meeting. Seeing their lawless deeds will not vex your soul.

Lot, on the other hand, chose to dwell near the wicked for his own benefit or pleasure. When you as a believer choose to watch a video with unrighteousness running through it, read a magazine bathed in the spirit of the world, or choose to go into a place of leisure or entertainment that has lawless deeds within it, you choose to vex your righteous soul. But even worse than that, you in essence disqualify yourself from the privilege of approaching the mountain of the Lord.

WHERE DO WE FIND REST FOR OUR SOULS?

You may protest, "But Jesus was able to eat with sinners." Yes, that is right. He went to the gatherings to reach out to them, which is what we are to do. But He did not go there to be entertained or relax. You may ask, "Then where can a believer go for relaxation?" Jesus went to a deserted place (Mark 6:31). This signifies a place away from the world's system.

My favorite place to rest used to be the beach. Now I rarely find a quiet beach. At most beaches people run around with less covering their bodies than their underwear, with the spirit of lust burning. (I wonder how the skimpy, tight-fitting bathing suits of today would have fared in the 1940s? They would have shocked conservative nonbelievers! I am not at all trying to be legalistic or old-fashioned, but I wonder if we are more connected as a subculture to the world than we realize?) Instead of the beach, I go to the mountains, heavily wooded areas, or lake areas for vacations. In these areas I can get away from the world's system and truly rest my soul.

Why do some believers have to be entertained or seek rest where the mannerisms and patterns of the world are most evident? Are we trying to get away from God's presence in our rest, or are we going to quiet ourselves so that we can enjoy His peaceful presence? Could it be that we have not realized the promise of His presence awaiting those who separate themselves and draw near?

Some of my remarks in this chapter were inspired by chapters 3 and 4 in David W. Bercot, *Will the Real Heretics Please Stand Up?* (Tyler, TX.: Scroll Publishing, 1989).

CHAPTER 9

SAVING GRACE

*Grace is depicted as the ability to live free of ungodliness and
worldly desires. It is the essence of the power to live
a life of holiness before God.*

The Old Testament certainly does not contain outdated Scriptures. On the contrary, Jesus says, "Do not think that I have come to abolish the Law or the Prophets; I have not come to abolish them but to fulfill them" (Matt. 5:17 NIV). How are we to know what He has fulfilled and still is fulfilling without understanding them? Now that we have developed a background from the Old Testament of God's desire to dwell among His people, let's return to Paul's statement in the new covenant:

Do not be unequally yoked together with unbelievers. For what fellowship has righteousness with lawlessness? And what communion has light with darkness? And what accord has Christ with Belial? Or what part has a believer with an unbeliever? And what agreement has the temple of God with idols? For you are the temple of the living God. As God has said:

"I will dwell in them
And walk among them.
I will be their God,
And they shall be My people." (2 Cor. 6:14–16 NKJV)

God makes three distinct promises. First, He will dwell in us and walk among us. Second, He will be our God. Third, we will be His people. These are His promises, yet they did not originate in the New Testament. Paul reiterates what the Lord repeatedly told Israel; His desires for us are the same. On one occasion His exact words to Israel were, "I will walk among you and be your God, and you shall be My people" (Lev. 26:12 NKJV). This has been His desire since the beginning.

As we have learned He is speaking of His desire to dwell among us in His glory. The Holy Spirit through the apostle Paul issues the same words to New Testament believers. Yet, as with Israel, there is a condition:

> Come out from among them
> And be separate, says the Lord.
> Do not touch what is unclean,
> And I will receive you.
> I will be a Father to you,
> And you shall be My sons and daughters,
> Says the LORD Almighty. (2 Cor. 6:17–18 NKJV)

The condition is no different from what it was for Moses and the children of Israel. We are to be separate from the world's system. If we obey, God will receive us and reveal Himself to us! But if we don't, our fate will be worse than it was for the Hebrews.

God told Moses to consecrate the people. Being set apart for Him would enable them to behold His glory. We are given the exact instruction to be separate. To paraphrase, God is saying, "I have delivered you from the world. Now get the world out of you!" Obeying will prepare us for His glory.

Moses was told to instruct Israel to "wash their clothes." They were to get the filth of Egypt off themselves. Even so we are told, "Therefore, having these promises, beloved, let us cleanse ourselves from all filthiness of the flesh and spirit, perfecting holiness in the fear of God" (2 Cor. 7:1 NKJV).

We are to perfect holiness by cleansing ourselves from the filth of the garments of the flesh and spirit. As with Israel, we are to wash the filth of the world off ourselves. Paul does not say, "God will cleanse you," or "The blood of Jesus will take care of cleansing you." The meaning is clearer in the original language. The Greek word for "perfecting" is *epiteleo*. Thayer's Greek dictionary defines this word as "to take upon oneself to bring to an end, to accomplish, to perfect, to execute, or to complete." That puts on us the responsibility of initiating and carrying out our purifying.

Of course, we could never do this without God's grace, for grace is His bestowed ability to do what His truth demands. It empowers us to obey God's words. That explains why Paul says,

> And working together with Him, we also urge you not to receive the grace of God in vain. (2 Cor. 6:1 NASB)

To receive something in vain would be not to use its potential. Let's say I lived near a volcanic mountain. An announcement is made that it will erupt in the next twenty-four hours. Without means of transportation I could in no way escape because I could not get far enough away from the mountain on foot in that twenty-four-hour period. Without an automobile I am doomed. In seeing my need a generous and loving person knocks on my door, gives me a car, puts the keys into my hand, and says, "The car is yours. You are now saved."

I rejoice that I have been saved. Being almost penniless, I never could have bought the automobile. This person has freely given me the automobile that is going to carry me to safety.

I call friends and excitedly tell them, "I have been saved! I am not going to die! A very compassionate person has given me an automobile to get out of this disaster. Isn't it wonderful?" I then dig out my maps, and I even buy a book telling me how to drive more proficiently.

However, for the next twenty-four hours I remain in the house. I fail to get into the car to drive to freedom. The volcano erupts, and I am swept away to destruction. The gift that would lead to my freedom was provided, but I just celebrated it and took no action. Afterward, all who knew my position and what I had received would say, "He received the automobile in vain."

In the same way, to receive God's grace in vain would mean that He has given us the power to walk free from the snares of this world through holiness, but we neglect it.

AN UNSCRIPTURAL GRACE

A deceptive thought process is present in our modern church. It has been conceived and brought forth by an unbalanced teaching of grace. Most often grace is referred to as an excuse or cover-up for a life of worldliness. To put it quite bluntly, it is used as a justification for self-seeking, fleshly lifestyles. Too many Christian groups have overemphasized the goodness of God to the neglect of His holiness and justice. This swing to the extreme left has caused many to have a warped understanding of the grace of God. Thus, many have received the grace of God in vain.

The grace of God is not merely a cover-up. Yes, it covers, but it goes beyond that: it enables and empowers us to live a life of obedience. In Jesus' Sermon on the Mount (Matt. 5 NKJV), He repeats these words: "You have heard that it was said to those of old . . . But I say to you . . ." (vv. 21–22). The pattern continues four more times to the end of the chapter (vv. 27–28, 31–32, 33–34, 43–44). What is He doing? Jesus quotes the requirement of the Law of Moses: "You have heard it said . . ." Then Jesus introduces what God seeks from a believer under the new covenant: "But I say to you . . ." He contrasts the Mosaic Law with grace and truth.

John says, "For the law was given through Moses, but grace and truth came through Jesus Christ" (John 1:17 NKJV). Jesus introduces the dimension of grace that will impart the ability of God within us that will free us from the dead formula of the law. The law is an outside restraint while grace is an inward transformation.

Often I hear believers and ministers bemoan the harsh requirements of the law, then express their relief that they are under grace and not such a rigid lifestyle. Well, I also rejoice exceedingly that I am no longer under the law. But it is not because I find God's standard of holiness more lenient now. The opposite is true. For I have found His standard higher under grace!

Let's delve deeper into the comparisons of Jesus in His Sermon on the Mount:

> You have heard that it was said to those of old, "You shall not murder, and whoever murders will be in danger of the judgment." But I say to you that whoever is angry with his brother without a cause shall be in danger of the judgment. And whoever says to his brother, "Raca!" shall be in danger of the council. But whoever says, "You fool!" shall be in danger of hell fire. (Matt. 5:21–22 NKJV)

The word *Raca* means "empty-headed." It was a term of reproach commonly used among Jews at the time of Christ. If anger reached the point where one called a brother a fool, Jesus said he was in danger of hell. The word *fool* means "godless." The fool has said in his heart there is no God (Ps. 14:1). Calling a brother a fool was a serious accusation. No one would say such a thing unless his anger had turned to hatred. Saying, "Raca," or "Fool," is comparable to one today saying, "I hate you," and meaning it.

In the Old Testament, a person was guilty of murder if he took a physical life. Under grace in the New Testament, God equates hating one's brother with the severity of committing murder: "Whoever hates his brother is a murderer, and you know that no murderer has eternal life abiding in him" (1 John 3:15 NKJV).

Under the law, you had to run a knife through someone to be guilty. Under grace, if you refuse to forgive or you allow prejudice or another form of hatred to rule your heart, it is evidence that God's grace does not abide in you or that you have neglected it, thus receiving it in vain. So is Jesus describing grace as the big "cover-up," or does He reveal it as His power, which enables us to live a holy life?

Here is another comparison that Jesus makes:

> You have heard that it was said to those of old, "You shall not commit adultery." But I say to you that whoever looks at a woman to lust [desire] for her has already committed adultery with her in his heart. (Matt. 5:27–28 NKJV)

A judgment of guilt was passed under the old covenant when an act of adultery was physically committed. In contrast, under the new covenant, God considers a man to be in adultery when he merely looks at a woman with desire in his heart for her. Under the law, you had to do it; under the new covenant of grace, all you have to do is *want* to do it! Does this sound like the grace we've lived and taught in America? Does this sound like the big cover-up, or God's given ability to live a holy life?

If grace is merely a cover-up, then it would appear that Jesus contradicts the very grace He came to impart. But this is not true: "For the grace of God that brings salvation has appeared to all men, teaching us that, denying ungodliness and worldly lusts, we should live soberly, righteously, and godly in the present age" (Titus 2:11–12 NKJV). Grace is depicted as the ability to live free of ungodliness and worldly desires. It is the essence of the power to live a life of holiness before God.

The writer of Hebrews exhorts us to "let us have grace, by which we may serve God acceptably with reverence and godly fear" (Heb. 12:28 NKJV). Again, *grace* is defined not as a cover-up but as a force that enables us to serve God acceptably. Grace that is received in vain results in an unchanged heart toward the impurities of the world. Therefore, the fruit of holiness is the proof of our salvation.

SAVED BY WORKS?

Some people may argue, "But the Bible says, 'By grace we have been saved through faith, not of our own works; it is the gift of God'" (Eph. 2:8–9, author's paraphrase).

Yes, this is true. It is impossible to live a life worthy of our inheritance in the kingdom of God in our own strength, for all have sinned and fallen short of God's righteous standard. No one will ever be able to stand before God and claim that his works, charitable deeds, or good life has earned him the right to inhabit His kingdom. Every one of us has transgressed and deserves to burn in the lake of fire eternally.

God's answer for our shortcomings is the gift of salvation through His gift of grace! A gift cannot be earned. Romans 4:4 (NKJV) asserts, "Now to him who works, the wages are not counted as grace but as debt." You cannot live a life good enough that you could deserve or buy it. You could pour out your life in sacrifice and charitable works, yet never earn this grace. It is a gift, and you receive it through faith in Jesus.

Let's complete the teaching and not stop short. Recall in our example of the person threatened by the volcanic mountain the car was given as a gift. It could not be bought; our subject did not have the money for it. Yet even though he received the gift, he still had to use its potential. His action or works of driving out of the territory would save him. Even so, none of us could buy our own grace. We have been given it as a gift, which we can never earn. But we must use its potential.

That is why James boldly states to believers: "Faith by itself, if it does not have works, is dead" (James 2:17 NKJV). James is not contradicting Paul. He is rounding out or clarifying Paul's message. He is pointing out that just as our friend would not have been saved if he did not drive the car, even so grace without corresponding works is of no effect. It has been received in vain.

He continues, "But someone will say, 'You have faith, and I have works.' Show me your faith without your works, and I will show you my faith by my works" (James 2:18 NKJV). James states that a life of holiness is the evidence a person has received God's gift of grace through faith. Grace, therefore, imparts the desire to obey and the ability to obey. That is why Paul says, "This is a faithful saying, and these things I want you to affirm constantly, that those who have believed in God should be careful to maintain good works" (Titus 3:8 NKJV). A professing believer who consistently disobeys God's Word has never truly received the grace of God, or he has received it in vain.

James emphasizes, "You see then that a man is justified by works, and not by faith only" (James 2:24 NKJV). Wow, what a statement! I dare say that few evangelical or charismatic believers are aware that this verse in the Bible exists.

A short while ago I opened a message by isolating this Scripture. It was very quiet in the auditorium after I read it. The people were so accustomed to a works-free message that it took a few moments for the meaning to sink in. Of course, I then read the verse in context, but their hearts were open and their attention secured.

James prefaces this statement by using Abraham, the father of faith, as the example:

> Was not Abraham our father justified by works [notice, justified by works] when he offered Isaac his son on the altar? Do you see that faith was working together with his works, and by works faith was made perfect [complete]? And the Scripture was fulfilled which says,

"Abraham believed God, and it was accounted to him for righteousness." (James 2:21–23 NKJV)

What Jesus Is Looking for in Us

Not long ago while I was in prayer the Lord conveyed statements so contrary to what has been taught in our churches that they startled me. In fact, I questioned whether it was really His voice. But I identified in the Scripture what He said to me.

Before I share the statements, I need to describe the subject matter. Early in the book of Revelation, Jesus gives seven different messages to seven churches. These are historic churches, but God never would have put these messages in Scripture if they did not have prophetic application. In other words, the messages still apply to us today.

The first statement that the Lord made to me in prayer was, "John, did you notice that the first words out of My mouth to every one of the seven churches in the book of Revelation were, 'I know your works'?" I found the following in the book of Revelation:

- *First Church:* To the angel [messenger] of the church of Ephesus write . . . I know your works. (Rev. 2:1–2 NKJV)
- *Second Church:* And to the angel of the church in Smyrna write . . . I know your works. (Rev. 2:8–9 NKJV)
- *Third Church:* And to the angel of the church in Pergamos write . . . I know your works. (Rev. 2:12–13 NKJV)
- *Fourth Church:* And to the angel of the church in Thyatira write . . . I know your works. (Rev. 2:18–19 NKJV)
- *Fifth Church:* And to the angel of the church in Sardis write . . . I know your works. (Rev. 3:1 NKJV)
- *Sixth Church:* And to the angel of the church in Philadelphia write . . . I know your works. (Rev. 3:7–8 NKJV)

- *Seventh Church:* And to the angel of the church of the Laodiceans write . . . I know your works. (Rev. 3:14–15 NKJV)

"I know your works" are the first words out of His mouth to all seven churches. I thought, *How have we gotten so far away from what He emphasizes and is looking for in us?*

While pondering this I heard the Lord utter the second statement, which was the one that riveted me: "John, did you notice that I did not say to one of those churches, 'I know your hearts'?"

I thought how many times I had sat in a counseling appointment with a professing believer who was leading a loose or worldly lifestyle and heard him say with firm conviction of innocence, "Well, God knows my heart!"

Jesus is not looking at our intentions, wishes, or knowledge of what is right. He is looking at our works! Are we allowing the grace of God to produce holy living in our lives, or have we received the grace of God in vain?

A Misunderstanding of the Word *Believe*

One reason we have strayed so far from the true meaning of grace is our incorrect teaching of the word *believe*. In our day this word has been reduced to a mental acknowledgment. Multitudes have prayed the sinner's prayer because they believe Jesus exists and they were emotionally moved by nonconfrontational messages lacking the call to repentance. But they have not turned from the lifestyle of seeking what the world seeks. They continue to live for themselves, trusting in an intellectual or emotional salvation that is not real.

In the Scriptures, *believe* means not only to acknowledge the existence of Jesus but also to obey His will and His Word. In Hebrews 5:9 (NKJV) we read, "And having been perfected, He became the author of eternal salvation to all who obey Him." To believe is to obey. The proof of Abraham's belief was in his corresponding works of obedience. Heeding the call to sanctification, he left his family, friends, and country. Later he offered what was most precious to him: his son. Nothing at all, not even his son, meant more to him than obeying God. That is true faith. That is why he is honored as "the father of us all" (Rom. 4:16 NKJV). Do we see this faith evident in the church today? How have we been so deceived?

Just saying that you have faith does not prove your salvation. How can faith be real without corresponding actions of obedience, which produce true holiness? Hear James's words again: "You see then that a man is justified by works, and not by faith only."

Not Everyone Who Says, "Lord, Lord"

We know a true believer not by what he confesses but by his "fruit to holiness" (Rom. 6:22 NKJV). Jesus clarifies this by saying, "Therefore by their fruits you will know them. Not everyone who says to Me, 'Lord, Lord,' shall enter the kingdom of heaven, but he who does the will of My Father in heaven" (Matt. 7:20–21 NKJV).

Allow me to put these words into modern vernacular: "You will know who is and isn't a believer not by what he professes, but by his submission to My Father's will. Not everyone who says, 'I am a Christian, and Jesus is my Lord,' will be granted entrance into heaven, but only those who obey the will of the Father."

Jesus says again, "Many will say to Me in that day, 'Lord, Lord, have we not prophesied in Your name, cast out demons in Your name, and done many wonders in Your name?' And then I will declare to them, 'I never knew you; depart from Me, you who practice lawlessness!'" (Matt. 7:22–23 NKJV).

In our modern vernacular: "A great number of people will confess Me as Lord and pray a sinner's prayer. Many of them consider themselves 'Full Gospel.' Yes, even those who did miracles and cast out demons in My name will be shocked at the realization on that day. They expect an entrance to the kingdom of heaven, only to hear Me say, 'Depart from Me, you who did not obey the will of My Father.'"

This is not my account or my words. It is not pleasant to think that many who professed His lordship will be denied admittance to the kingdom of heaven. Yes, even those who cast out demons and did miracles in His name!

Some commentators have tried to reason that Jesus refers to people who have never received Him. However, this interpretation is incorrect, for those who have never professed salvation in Jesus' name cannot do supernatural works in His name. An account of those who tried appeared in the book of Acts. The seven sons of Sceva took it upon themselves to call the name of the Lord Jesus over those who had evil spirits, saying, "We exorcise you by the Jesus whom Paul preaches." The evil spirit who was in the man answered and said, "'Jesus I know, and Paul I know; but who are you?' Then the man in whom the evil spirit was leaped on them, overpowered them, and prevailed against them, so that they fled out of that house naked and wounded" (Acts 19:13–16 NKJV).

While in prayer I received a sobering spiritual vision in the late 1980s. I saw a multitude of people, too great to number, the magnitude of which I had never seen before. They were amassed before the gates of heaven, awaiting entrance, expecting to hear the Master say, "Come, you blessed of My Father, inherit the kingdom prepared for you from the foundation of the world" (Matt. 25:34 NKJV). But instead they heard the Master say, "I never knew you; depart from Me."

You may question, "If Jesus said He had never known them, how could they cast out devils and do miracles in His name?" The answer is that these men and women join themselves with Jesus for the benefits of salvation. Though they accept Him in order to be saved, as with the children of Israel, they do not come to know the heart of God; they go only as far as His provision. They seek Him for their own benefit; their service is self-motivated, not love-motivated.

In Jesus' statement "I never knew you," the English word *knew* is the Greek word *ginosko*. In the New Testament it is used to describe intercourse between a man and a woman (Matt. 1:25); it represents intimacy. Jesus is actually saying, "I never intimately knew you." Moses intimately knew God, but Israel knew Him only by the miracles He did in their lives. This is no different.

We read in 1 Corinthians 8:3 (NKJV), "But if anyone loves God, this one is known by Him." The word *known* is the same Greek word *ginosko*. God intimately knows those who love Him. They have laid their lives down for Him (John 15:13). Only those who do this can keep His Word. Jesus points to this truth: "He who does not love Me does not keep My words" (John 14:24 NKJV).

The true evidence of love for Jesus is not what is said but what is lived. John explains,

> We know that we have come to know him if we obey his commands. The man who says, "I know him," but does not do what he commands is a liar [he's deceived], and the truth is not in him. But if anyone obeys his word, God's love is truly made complete in him. This is how we know we are in him. (1 John 2:3–5 NIV)

Judas joined himself with Jesus. He seemed to love Him, and he dropped everything to follow Him. Judas stayed with Jesus despite the heat of persecution, not quitting when other disciples did (John 6:66). He cast out devils, healed the sick, and preached the gospel. Yes, it is written that Jesus "called His twelve disciples together and gave them power and authority over all demons, and to cure diseases. He sent them to preach the kingdom of God and to heal the sick" (Luke 9:1–2 NKJV). It does not cite the eleven disciples; Judas is included.

However, Judas's motive was not right from the beginning. He never repented of his self-seeking ways. His character is revealed by saying, "What are you willing to give me if I . . . ?" (Matt. 26:15 NKJV).

He lied and deceived to gain advantage (Matt. 26:25), he took money from the treasury of Jesus' ministry for personal use (John 12:4–6), and the disreputable list goes on. He never knew Jesus, even though he spent three and a half years in His company!

How many today are like Judas? They have made sacrifices for the ministry, preached the gospel, and possibly operated in the gifts of the Spirit, yet have not intimately known Him. All their labor is conceived from self-serving motives.

Jesus asks, "But why do you call Me 'Lord, Lord,' and not do the things which I say?" (Luke 6:46 NKJV). "Lord" in this verse originates from the Greek word *kurios*. Strong's dictionary of Greek words defines it as "supreme in authority or master." Jesus explains that many will confess Him as Lord, but He is not their supreme authority. They live in a manner that does not support what they confess; they obey the will of God when it does not conflict with the desires of their own hearts. If the will of God takes them a different direction from the one they desire, they choose their own path, yet still call Jesus "Lord."

Often success in ministry is measured purely by numbers. This mentality has caused many to do whatever was necessary to fill their altars with "converts" and the church with "members." To accomplish this, they have preached Jesus as Savior but not as Lord. The underlying message has been, "Come to Jesus and get salvation, peace, love, joy, prosperity, success, health, and more!" Yes, Jesus is the fulfillment of all these promises, but the benefits have been so overemphasized that the pure gospel is reduced to an answer to life's problems now, followed with a guarantee of heaven.

This type of preaching merely entices sinners. They hear a message of coming to God, void of repentance: "Give God a chance. He will give you love, peace, and joy!" In doing this, we bypass repentance to gain a "convert." Converts join the church, but what kind are they? Jesus confronted the ministers of His day: "You travel over land and sea to win a single convert, and when he becomes one, you make him twice as much a son of hell as you are" (Matt. 23:15 NIV). Converts are easily made, but are they men and women with hearts after God or the promises? We have seen the difference between Moses and the children of Israel.

Jesus made it clear to the multitude, "If anyone would come after me, he must deny himself and take up his cross and follow me. For whoever wants to save his life will lose it, but whoever loses his life for me and for the gospel will save it" (Mark 8:34–35 NIV). All you have to do is to "want" to save your life, and you will lose it. And He did not say, "Whoever wants to lose his life for My sake." Just "wanting" to lose your life is not enough. Jesus is not looking for good intentions.

The rich young ruler wanted passionately to be saved. He came running to Jesus and knelt before Him, crying out for eternal life. Yet his emotional desire was not enough. Jesus said to him, "You lack something" (*see* Mark 10:17–22). The young man walked away when he realized the price of the Cross. At least, we can respect his honesty!

Thousands who do not attend church would gladly receive the benefits of salvation if only they could keep control of their lives. Somehow they seem to realize what many in the church have missed. You pay a price to serve God. They are honest with God; they don't want to pay it. On the other hand there are those who are deceived. They attend church, call Jesus "Lord," and declare their submission to His lordship, while in reality they have not submitted.

TWO DIFFERENT MESSAGES

I hope you now see the difference between the grace Jesus preaches and the one we've believed. The present-day message of grace often extols, "Believe in Jesus, pray the sinner's prayer, confess Him as your Savior, and then you will enter the kingdom of heaven." There is little mention of denying self and the world. Then, once people are in church, little is said about the power that grace gives for us to live holy lives.

After people are converted and taught in this manner, any unholy living or disobedience is believed to be covered by the carte blanche grace of God. Could this condition be the reason for the lack of God's fire and His power in our churches?

I hope you hear this message in the spirit it has been delivered. I love God's people and desire for them to prosper as their souls prosper. Therefore, I am compelled to proclaim His truth. I know teaching and doctrine shape an individual's belief and life. My heart breaks for the multitude in the churches who have been lulled into a lukewarm state, lacking His fire.

Paul instructed Timothy, "Watch your life and doctrine closely. Persevere in them, because if you do, you will save both yourself and your hearers" (1 Tim. 4:16 NIV). We must heed this warning. Perverted truth may sound good and even appeal to our sense of reason, but it will lead to deception.

The truth of God's Word will feed and build you up. It will train you to discern between correct and incorrect thinking. Perverted truth can disqualify you. That is why God admonishes us to give His Word full attention that we might correctly handle it. This chapter bears both warning and encouragement. The warning: don't allow incorrect doctrines of grace to disqualify you by receiving it in vain. The encouragement: there is the strength to live a sanctified life through the grace of God. May the grace of our Lord Jesus Christ be with you.

CHAPTER 10

DIFFICULT DAYS

*Out of this love for Him comes fire that
fuels their passion. They delight in obeying Him.*

"Pursue . . . holiness, without which no one will see the Lord:
looking carefully lest anyone fall short of the grace of God."
—*Hebrews 12:14–15 NKJV*

Without holiness no one will see the Lord. Have we really believed these words, or have they just been a good quote from the Bible? Has the church viewed them as a command or merely a motivating poetic statement to help us aim for an ideal lifestyle, which is certainly unattainable in this day or hour? And what could the writer of Hebrews possibly mean by "looking carefully lest anyone fall short of the grace of God"? How could anyone fall short of the grace of God that has been taught in the majority of our churches the past twenty-five years? Could this just be an "overkill" statement from God to make us afraid and keep us out of trouble? Absolutely not!

UNCHANGED BELIEVERS

As I stated in the last chapter, for too many people, grace has been represented as the big cover-up, which has absolved believers from just about any responsibility to walk in obedience and holiness. But this belief again is proved to be scripturally in error by this statement, for to fall short of the grace of God is not to walk in its potential. It is to receive God's gift of grace in vain by remaining unchanged.

Paul foresaw this condition of remaining unchanged in numerous professing believers of these last days. In describing these days he says they will be "difficult times." It's interesting to hear him refer to our day of religious freedom as difficult when he was stoned, beaten with rods, chained, imprisoned, and whipped for his firm stance on the gospel. Yet he writes that our day will be difficult because many professing believers in the Lord Jesus will still love themselves and their money and will seek pleasure more passionately than God. Some will be proud; others unthankful; still others unforgiving. Among believers will be those who are disobedient and unholy, and many who will lack self-control. Others will be headstrong.

Paul says these men and women will have a form of Christianity, "but they will reject the power that could make them godly" (2 Tim. 3:1–5 NLT). They have not allowed the power of grace to change them from being lovers of money and pleasure to lovers of God and people. They have remained unholy and have received the grace of God in vain.

He then goes on to say that these unchanged "believers" will be "always learning and never able to come to the knowledge of the truth" (v. 7 NKJV). Today we have had more Christian teaching in America than at any other time in history and in any other nation. Billions of dollars have been spent on communicating the gospel through books, tapes, videos, television sets, satellite links, not to mention numerous church services and conferences. Yet we have grown into a worldly church that has not separated itself from the desires of Egypt. Paul describes as difficult not his day of physical persecution but our day of a worldly church!

At lunch with a minister friend, I learned about his trip to a nation in Africa that is predominantly Muslim. Currently they are torturing and putting to death Christians there. He told me of meeting men who had been tortured, yet they still had the passion to continue to preach the gospel to their countrymen. As my friend went to preach to the believers each day he drove past the gallows used for Christians. He said, "John, I wonder how many Americans would continue to go to church if they daily drove by the place where they may be hung for their belief?" Then he made a comment that agrees with what Paul says. He said, "John, in America we have religious freedom, which they don't have. But they have spiritual freedom, which we don't have in America."

According to Paul, in the last days difficult times will not come because of the persecution of the saints but rather because of the worldliness of the church. Could it be that we have misused our freedom?

At a conference where I was a speaker, I sat across the table from a minister who had just returned from visiting a communist country in Asia. The persecution is so severe that believers hold meetings in secret. The pastor who organized the meetings and his leaders had been arrested numerous times. In prison they continued to preach the gospel to jailed criminals, and many were saved. The authorities were so angry that they put the leaders and the pastor in solitary confinement. The pastor had been arrested more than one hundred times and had spent a total of more than ten years in prison.

Their services went undisturbed until the last one. The police discovered where they were meeting, and had it not been for their lookouts, they would have been arrested. Before they broke up they agreed to meet in a remote place very early the next morning before this minister was scheduled to leave. The next morning they showed up and wanted prayer. She told me, "John, I felt that they should have prayed for me, not me for them. But I knew God would honor their faith." At the end of the last meeting the pastor began to weep. When she asked why, he responded that he was concerned for his people. With tears in his eyes he said, "I fear our freedom."

This minister was baffled. "Why do you fear your freedom?" she replied. "You have been hunted, persecuted, and imprisoned many times. Think of all you could do if you and your people were free."

He continued, "I fear that these men and women will become materialistic and worldly if they have their freedom and will fall away as some others in the Western church."

How could she argue with him, seeing his pure devotion to God and to the people he oversaw? Was this the typical dedication she had encountered in the Western world? We view these persecuted saints as having difficult days, but who, according to the Scripture, is having difficult times? Paul says that we who have religious freedom but a worldly church will have the difficult days.

Religious freedom has not made us worldly, though it has created an atmosphere to cultivate the already-existing desires within us that have pulled us away. Our true problem, as with Israel of old, is our lack of passion for God's glory. And as with Israel, this problem stems from our attraction to pleasure and our fleshly appetites.

JESUS' MESSAGE TO HIS CHURCH IN THE LAST DAYS

In the last chapter, we discussed briefly seven letters to historic churches in the book of Revelation that hold prophetic messages. Many theologians agree that the seven churches represent a chronological pattern of the church at large, progressing from the early church in the first few centuries to the one just before the Lord's second coming.

Though we do not know the day or the hour of the Lord's second coming, Jesus says we will know the season. Most scholars agree that we are living in the season of His return. Therefore, the exhortation to the last church, Laodicea, applies prophetically to us: "And to the angel of the church of the Laodiceans write, 'These things says the Amen, the Faithful and True Witness, the Beginning of the creation of God'" (Rev. 3:14 NKJV).

Jesus calls Himself the Faithful and True Witness. "Faithful" means He is consistent and constant. "True" means He will speak only the truth, even if it is not delightful. "Faithful" and "True" mean he will be consistently true, no matter what the reaction or pressure.

A false witness will lie and flatter. He will tell you only what you want to hear at the expense of what you need to hear. Dishonest salesmen want your money and will treat you well and tell you just what you want to hear. But their motive is to take from you. As a church, we have embraced ministers who have told us what we wanted to hear. We wanted to hear only nice and wonderful things to the neglect of the truth we've needed.

Jesus comforts and builds, but not at the terrible expense of neglecting to tell you the truth. He loves and forgives but also chastens and corrects! Hear His words: "I know your works, that you are neither cold nor hot" (Rev. 3:15 NKJV).

He says "works," not "intentions." The road to hell is paved with good intentions. How does He know their condition? The answer again is clear: by their works, or actions.

The actions of ones who are cold blatantly disobey God. They do not pretend to be something they are not; they are lost and know it. They know they are not serving God. They serve other gods, their money, their businesses, themselves. They live for the pleasure of the moment, in revelry and riot. It is the life of a sinner or the admitted backslider.

On the other hand, ones who are hot are consumed with God. They have purified themselves so that they can draw close to His presence. Holiness is their passion; without it they know they cannot see the Lord. Jesus encompasses their hearts and beings. Out of this love for Him comes fire that fuels their passion. They delight in obeying Him. They also know their true condition.

Jesus warns the last church that their condition is neither cold nor hot. Then He says, "I could wish you were cold or hot" (Rev. 3:15 NKJV).

The meaning of this statement eluded me for years. Why does Jesus say to a church, "I would rather you be cold or hot"? Why doesn't He say, "I wish you were hot"? He never speaks dishonestly or with exaggeration, so their present condition (of somewhere between cold and hot) has to be worse than cold. How can all-out sinners or acknowledged backsliders be in a better position than these "church believers"?

He answers this with His next statement: "So then, because you are lukewarm, and neither cold nor hot, I will vomit you out of My mouth" (Rev. 3:16 NKJV). Lukewarm has too much hot to be cold and too much cold to be hot. It has enough heat to blend in undetected with the hot and enough cool to slip in unnoticed with the cold. Lukewarm people become like whoever they are around. Around true followers of Jesus, they can blend in with them. They know the Scriptures, sing the songs, and say the right statements.

Around followers of the world, they might not drink or smoke, but they think and conduct their lives in a worldly manner, that is, selfishly. They obey God when obedience is pleasant or in their best interests. But they are really motivated by their own desires.

Jesus says, "I will vomit you out of My mouth." Why does He choose this graphic analogy? We vomit what the body cannot assimilate. For lunch one day years ago, my second- and third-born sons ordered hamburgers. Within the hour both of them had vomited their lunch, which had been made from bad meat. Their bodies rejected it because it was harmful to assimilate. The "bad" hamburgers looked just like the "good" ones they had eaten at other times. Jesus is actually saying, "I am going to vomit out of My body those who say they belong to Me, but in reality don't."

Neither the cold nor the hot are deceived concerning their relationship with God, but lukewarm people are deceived. They think their condition is something other than what it is. They think they belong to Jesus. That is why it could be worse for them than for all-out sinners. Sinners know they are not serving God; therefore they are easier to reach. Lukewarm people think they are serving God. They confess salvation by grace but have fallen short of the very grace of God they confess. They are much more difficult to reach.

If people think they are saved, they see no need for salvation. Jesus goes into detail about their true condition: "Because you say, 'I am rich, have become wealthy, and have need of nothing'—and do not know that you are wretched, miserable, poor, blind, and naked" (Rev. 3:17 NKJV).

The people in this church boasted in their wealth and lack of need. They comforted themselves with what they believed were God's blessings. Could this be a picture of the American church? Have we used our freedom and wealth to enhance our service to God? Or have we allowed our freedom and wealth to deceive us? With most in the Western church it has been the latter.

However, I have met faithful people in the Western church with a hot passion for God who have pursued holiness. They are a minority, not a majority. They are true soldiers who have seen the battleground and know their enemy. Their passion is evident by their fruit, not just their words.

Jesus declares to those who are lukewarm in the church: "I advise you to buy gold from me—gold that has been purified by fire. Then you will be rich. And also buy white garments so you will not be shamed by your nakedness. And buy ointment for your eyes so you will be able to see" (Rev. 3:18 NLT).

He emphasizes buying something from Him that obviously is not obtained by merely acknowledging His lordship. Remember, the church professed salvation in His name. Yet they lacked something that true believers are expected to possess. But how do we buy something from Jesus?

God says to us in Proverbs 23:23 (NKJV), "Buy the truth, and do not sell it." Through Isaiah the prophet, He says,

> Ho! Everyone who thirsts,
> Come to the waters;
> And you who have no money,
> Come, buy and eat. (Isa. 55:1 NKJV)

As in Jesus' statement, the focus is on purchasing something that money cannot buy.

Jesus speaks of the kingdom of heaven to His disciples: "The kingdom of heaven is like a merchant seeking beautiful pearls, who, when he had found one pearl of great price, went and sold all that he had and bought it" (Matt. 13:45–46 NKJV). To purchase this expensive pearl, which represents the kingdom, the person had to sell everything to have enough to buy it. In other words, give your entire life to serve Him and His cause without holding anything back for yourself; live completely for Him. Paul put it this way: "He died for all, that those who live should live no longer for themselves, but for Him who died for them and rose again" (2 Cor. 5:15 NKJV).

THE WISE AND THE FOOLISH

Some of Jesus' other parables illustrate this point. One is found in the first twelve verses of Matthew 25. The kingdom of heaven is compared to ten virgins who took their lamps and went out to meet the Bridegroom, Jesus. All of them were virgins, and they all called Him "Lord." All of them had lamps, which speak of light, representing those who have received the gift of eternal life. All of them were expecting to go with Him in His second coming. He is not talking about those who have not heard the gospel or never acknowledged belief in Him. In other words, He is not talking about the cold!

Of the ten virgins, five were wise and five were foolish. The ratio is significant. Jesus is discussing a sizable portion of the church.

What separated the wise from the foolish? The foolish had only their lamps. The wise had vessels that contained a surplus of oil to continually keep the lamps burning. At midnight a cry was heard that the Bridegroom was coming, and the virgins were to meet Him. But the lamps of the foolish were going out. They immediately said to the wise, "Give us some of your oil, for our lamps are going out" (v. 8 NKJV).

The wise answered them, "No, lest there should not be enough for us and you; but go rather to those who sell, and buy for yourselves" (v. 9 NKJV).

I had heard different ministers expound on this parable, yet I felt that I had not connected to the true meaning. Then one morning while I was outside in a remote place praying, I fervently cried out, "Lord, please help me understand this parable!"

That very day God showed me that the key statement of the parable is in the words of the wise virgins to the foolish: "But go rather to those who *sell*, and *buy* for yourselves." Picture this: ten virgins, five wise and five foolish, walk into a surplus store. The foolish walk up to the counter, pull out some money, and say to the clerk, "Give me one of those lamps. I want to be saved. I don't want to go to hell. I want the blessings of God." Each leaves the counter with a lamp that is burning and says, "Thank God, I am saved!"

The wise walk up to the counter and pull out of their pockets all of their cash. They have liquidated every asset and brought that money as well as their savings. They say to the clerk, "That represents everything I own, every penny I am worth. I have nothing else! Please give me that lamp, and use every penny left over to buy all the oil it will buy." Each one walks away with a lamp and a large vessel filled with oil to fuel the lamp.

The difference is that the wise gave their entire lives and the foolish gave only what they thought was required to be saved. They kept back part of their lives. Though they left with a lamp that burned and their light could be seen, it would not endure to the end. In the parable their lamps began to go out at midnight. In the darkest hour, when tribulation hit its peak, they could no longer endure. That is why Jesus often says, "He who endures to the end shall be saved."

The foolish virgins immediately went out to buy, but while they were gone, the Bridegroom came. The wise who were ready went with Him to the wedding, and the door was shut. Upon their return, the foolish cried out, "Lord, Lord, open to us!" (v. 11 NKJV). But He answered and said, "Assuredly, I say to you, I do not know you" (v. 12 NKJV).

Again the Lord utters, "I do not know you," to those who confess His lordship. The lukewarm had not given their entire lives. These words of Jesus surely applied to them: "He who does not take his cross and follow after Me is not worthy of Me" (Matt. 10:38 NKJV).

Why have we believed a gospel in America that has given us the provisions of resurrection power without the Cross? This gospel has led us into a lukewarm state. It has robbed us of the fire of God that we need to burn in our hearts. Have we looked for the living among the dead? Have we forgotten His words, which so clearly state, "If you try to keep your life for yourself, you will lose it. But if you give up your life for me, you will find true life" (Matt. 16:25 NLT)?

CHAPTER 11

GOLD, GARMENTS, AND OINTMENT

The work of holiness is a
cooperative effort between the Deity and us.

"I advise you to buy gold from me—gold that has been purified by fire. Then you will be rich. And also buy white garments so you will not be shamed by your nakedness. And buy
ointment for your eyes so you will be able to see."
—*Revelation 3:18* NLT

Jesus urges those who lack a heart ablaze for Him to buy three
things: gold, white garments, and ointment for the eyes. Let's look
at each separately.

GOLD REFINED BY FIRE

The prophet Malachi tells us that in the last days the Lord is going to
come to His church as a refiner's fire: "He will sit and judge like a
refiner of silver, watching closely as the dross is burned away. He will
purify the Levites, refining them like gold or silver, so that they may
once again offer acceptable sacrifices to the LORD" (Mal. 3:3 NLT).

The word *Levites* prophetically refers to the "royal priesthood"
(1 Peter 2:9 NKJV), which, as we discussed earlier, is the church. This

prophet did not have New Testament terminology. He was not able to say, "He will purify the Christians," because that term had not been given yet. Since God compares the refinement of this priesthood with the refinement process for gold and silver, we must understand the characteristics of gold and silver and how they are refined. Jesus focuses on gold, so we will too.

Gold is widely distributed in nature but always in small quantities. Rarely is gold found in a pure state. In its purest form, gold is soft, pliable, and free from corrosion or other substances. When gold is mixed with other metals (for example, copper, iron, or nickel), it becomes harder, less pliable, and more corrosive. This mixture is called an alloy. The higher the percentage of copper, iron, nickel, or other metal, the harder the gold becomes. Conversely, the lower the percentage of alloy, the softer and more flexible it is.

Immediately we see Jesus' parallel: a pure heart before God is like pure gold, which has been refined. A pure heart is soft, tender, and pliable. Paul warns that the heart is hardened through the deceitfulness of sin (Heb. 3:13). Sin, which is disobedience to God's ways or authority, is the added substance that turns our pure gold into an alloy, hardening our hearts. This lack of tenderness creates a loss of sensitivity, which hinders our ability to hear His voice. Unfortunately, too many in the church have a form of godliness without a tender heart. Their hearts no longer burn for Jesus. That white-hot love for God has been replaced with a frigid self-love, which seeks only its own pleasure, comfort, and benefit. Supposing godliness is a means to personal gain (1 Tim. 6:5), they seek only the benefits of the promises and exclude the Promiser Himself. Deceived, they delight themselves with the world, expecting to receive heaven too. They are the lukewarm within the church. However, James admonishes that pure Christianity is to "keep oneself unspotted from the world" (James 1:27 NKJV). Jesus is coming for a church that is pure, without spot, or any impurity (Eph. 5:27), a church whose heart is unpolluted by the world's system!

Another characteristic of gold is its resistance to rust or corrosion. Even though other metals tarnish as a result of atmospheric changes, changes in the atmosphere do not tarnish pure gold. Brass (a yellow alloy of copper and zinc), though it resembles gold, does not behave as gold. Brass tarnishes easily. It has gold's appearance without possessing its character. The higher the percentage of foreign substance in gold, the more susceptible it is to corrosion and corruption.

Presently, the world's system has leached into the church. We have become infiltrated by its mannerisms, and we are tarnishing. In the Western church our values are polluted with worldliness. We have pursued our carnal appetites and called them the blessings of God. Thinking ourselves to be rich in these blessings, we have become insensitive and do not realize the need for purification.

Malachi shows that Jesus will refine His church, purge it of the influence of the world, just as a refiner purifies gold. In the refining process, gold is ground into powder and then mixed with a substance called flux. The two are then placed in a furnace and melted by an intense fire. The impurities are drawn by the flux and rise to the surface. The gold, which is heavier, remains at the bottom. The impurities, or dross (such as the copper, iron, or zinc combined with flux), are then removed.

Hear what God says through Isaiah the prophet: "I have refined you but not in the way silver [or gold] is refined. Rather, I have refined you in the furnace of suffering" (Isa. 48:10 NLT). The furnace He uses to refine us is affliction, hardship, or suffering, not a literal, physical fire as that with which silver or gold is refined. Peter affirms this by saying:

> In this you greatly rejoice, though now for a little while, if need be, you have been grieved by various trials, that the genuineness of your faith, being much more precious than gold that perishes, though it is tested by fire, may be found to praise, honor, and glory at the revelation of Jesus Christ. (1 Peter 1:6–7 NKJV)

The Lord's fire for refining is trials and tribulations. Their heat separates our impurities from the character of God in our lives.

I was brought up in a denominational church that taught all you needed to be saved was to be sprinkled with water as a baby, attend services, and keep the laws of the church. When I was saved in my fraternity in college in 1979, I was shortly afterward led to an independent church majoring on the blessings of God. Holiness was not taught in this church or in my denominational background.

In 1985 God began to deal with me in prayer about the need for purity, which created a hunger in my life. I passionately asked Him to purify my life. After several months, He responded. In December of that year He told me that He was going to teach me how to deny myself, take up my cross, and follow Him. He showed me that He was going to do a work of sanctification in my life.

Excitedly I told my wife, "God is going to remove all my impurities." I proceeded to tell her all the undesirable things God would be removing. Most were excesses, such as gluttonous eating patterns, too much television, and too much focus on pleasure. But for the next three months, nothing happened. As a matter of fact, things got worse. It was as if I had become twice as fleshly.

I asked the Lord, "Why are my bad habits getting worse, not better?"

He responded, "Son, I said I was going to purify you. You have been trying to do it in your own strength. Now I will do it My way."

From that point, I went through intense trials, such as I had never before experienced! And in the midst of them, God seemed to be millions of miles away, though He wasn't. Previously hidden personality flaws surfaced, and the root of these flaws could be summed up in one word—*selfishness!* I was rude and harsh with those closest to me. I sometimes yelled at my wife and children for no reason. I complained about almost everything. I was no fun to be around. I was unloving with my family, friends, and pastor, treating them all as if they were the reason for my anguish of soul. They began to avoid me because of my attitude and behavior.

Finally, I cried out to the Lord, "Where is all this anger coming from? It wasn't here before!"

He showed me in the Scripture His words on purification, then He responded to my question, "Son, when they purify gold, they put it into a very hot furnace, and the intense fire causes it to become liquid. Once this happens the impurities show up at the surface."

He directed me to look at my gold wedding band. It is a 14 karat gold ring, which means that 14 parts out of 24 parts are gold, but 10 parts are other metals. So it is roughly 60 percent gold.

Then He asked me the following questions that changed my life: "Does that ring look like pure gold to you?"

I answered, "Yes."

He said, "But it is not pure gold, is it?"

I replied, "No, Sir."

He continued, "You can't see the impurities in the gold before it is put in the fire, but that doesn't mean they are not there."

I responded by saying, "Yes, Lord."

Then He made this statement, which impacted my heart like a bomb: "When I put My fire under you, those impurities surfaced; though hidden to you, they were visible to Me. Now the choice is yours; your reaction to what has been exposed will determine your future. You can remain angry and blame your wife, friends, pastor, or the people you work with for your condition, thus allowing the impurities to stay due to the justification of your behavior. Later, when trials subside, they will be hidden once again. Or you can see your condition for what it is, repent, and ask forgiveness, and I'll take My ladle and remove those impurities from your life."

God does not remove them against our will. Paul knew that and thus urges us, "Let us cleanse ourselves from all filthiness of the flesh and spirit, perfecting holiness in the fear of God" (2 Cor. 7:1 NKJV). And to Timothy he wrote on this subject:

"Let everyone who names the name of Christ depart from iniquity." But in a great house there are not only vessels of gold and silver, but also of wood and clay, some for honor and some for dishonor. Therefore if anyone cleanses himself from the latter, he will be a vessel for honor, sanctified and useful for the Master, prepared for every good work. (2 Tim. 2:19–21 NKJV)

The work of holiness is a cooperative effort between the Deity and us. He supplies the grace, but we must be willing to ask for His purification. Then once He begins the process, we must cooperate through humility and obedience. In my life, I could see only the outward excesses of too much eating, television, pleasures, and so on. Yet God could see the deeper roots, and after He dealt with them, the others came back into line. Purification is a constant, ongoing, and often painful process, but knowing its yield, I welcome it.

Another characteristic of gold, in its purest state, is its transparency: "And the street of the city was pure gold, like transparent glass" (Rev. 21:21 NKJV). When you are purified by the fiery trials, you become transparent! A transparent vessel brings no glory to itself, but it glorifies what it contains. The more we are refined, the clearer the world can see Jesus in us. Hallelujah!

David, who had a heart after God, cried out, "Who can understand his errors? Cleanse me from secret faults" (Ps. 19:12 NKJV). Let this be our cry. If we ask God to purify our hearts, He will remove the impurities hidden from our eyes. God knows our innermost thoughts and intents, even though we may not. Refinement strengthens what is already good and cleanses or removes what weakens or defiles. For this reason Jesus counsels the church of this day to buy from Him gold refined in the fire that we might be rich, not with what the world pursues but with what endures eternally.

WHITE GARMENTS

After counseling this church to buy refined gold, Jesus advises them to buy from Him white garments, so that their nakedness may not be revealed. God exhorts Israel in similar terms when Isaiah cries out:

> Awake, awake!
> Put on your strength, O Zion;
> Put on your beautiful garments,
> O Jerusalem, the holy city! (Isa. 52:1 NKJV)

Zion is a type of the church. God does not say, "I will put your garments on you"; rather, you "put on your beautiful garments." Paul in a similar manner urges the church, "Clothe yourselves with the Lord Jesus Christ, and do not think about how to gratify the desires of the sinful nature" (Rom. 13:14 NIV). These pleas are offered because no one will come near the Lord without these white garments (Rev. 7:9). However, the key point with all three is that we must put them on.

Again, His grace provides the ability for us to purchase these garments. We could not have provided them for ourselves, for all our righteousness is as filthy rags (Isa. 64:6). But as the prophet says,

> I will greatly rejoice in the LORD,
> My soul shall be joyful in my God;
> For He has clothed me with the garments of salvation,
> He has covered me with the robe of righteousness,
> As a bridegroom decks himself with ornaments,
> And as a bride adorns herself with her jewels. (Isa. 61:10 NKJV)

The Lord provides the garment of salvation and the jewels to wear; we never could have furnished them for ourselves. But once again, these provisions can be received in vain. The bride must adorn herself.

Consider this example: a poor woman is asked to marry a great king's son. She is broke and has no means of obtaining any money to prepare herself for her wedding. She has only rags, and she cannot be permitted into the king's court with anything other than the proper attire. In his great love the king's son gives what is needed to buy a beautiful garment and jewels for her to wear on the wedding day. Yet she does nothing with the provision for the wedding; she spends it on her own pleasure. It is an insult to this great king and his son when she comes to the wedding without her proper garment. The ability to obtain the garment was graciously given to her, yet she received the provision in vain. She did not prepare herself for the wedding.

If she had used what he gave her to purchase her wedding garment, then her boast would have been in the king. She would have declared, "He has clothed me with this wedding garment." Through his gift of grace, she was able to clothe herself. It would have been completely his provision. However, she would have had to make herself ready by purchasing the garment and putting it on.

This example closely relates to our preparation for the return of our Bridegroom. John describes the scene he saw and heard:

> "Let us be glad and rejoice and give Him glory, for the marriage of the Lamb has come, and His wife [the church] has made herself ready." And to her it was granted to be arrayed in fine linen, clean and bright, for the fine linen is the righteous acts of the saints. (Rev. 19:7–8 NKJV)

The Greek word for "righteous acts" in verse 8 is *dikaioma*. Strong's dictionary defines this word as "an equitable deed." According to Vine's dictionary, this word signifies "an act of righteousness, a concrete expression of righteousness." God has given us His grace to produce works of righteousness. According to Scripture, these acts purchase the white garments with which we are to clothe ourselves for the wedding feast. Yet have we received His grace in vain? If our righteous works produce our wedding garments, then many of us are going to be found almost naked! Most in the Western church don't have enough works for a miniskirt, let alone a wedding garment! Again this explains and confirms James's bold statement (worded as a question), "But do you want to know, O foolish man, that faith without works is dead?" (James 2:20 NKJV). How have we lost sight of this truth in the modern Western church?

James provides two examples that illustrate true faith. He states: "Was not Abraham our father justified by works when he offered Isaac his son on the altar?" Someone may say, "I thought we were justified by faith." We are. But not the faith and grace that have been taught in the Western world during the last part of the twentieth century. Faith is not real unless there are corresponding works, and without His grace there could not be corresponding works. James continues,

> Do you see that faith was working together with his works, and by works faith was made perfect? And the Scripture was fulfilled which says, "Abraham believed God, and it was accounted to him for righteousness." And he was called the friend of God. You see then that a man is justified by works, and not by faith only. (James 2:21–24 NKJV)

In the second illustration, James writes, "Likewise, was not Rahab the harlot also justified by works when she received the messengers and sent them out another way? For as the body without the spirit is dead, so faith without works is dead also" (James 2:25–26 NKJV). Another translation says, "So faith without deeds is dead" (NIV).

Faith is not faith at all unless it is accompanied by works. We can proclaim our faith, as the Laodicean church did, but do we have corresponding hot works to confirm this faith?

Let's consider two parables that Jesus relates immediately after the parable of the ten virgins. Recall the point of the parable of the ten virgins is that the foolish did not give their entire lives, yet they still called Jesus "Lord." They were denied admittance to the wedding.

The next parable concerns a wealthy man going on a long trip. The wealthy man represents Jesus. He called together his servants and gave them money to invest for him while he was gone. He gave them differing amounts, according to their abilities, and then left. Two of the servants diligently worked and doubled what was given to them. The third, who was given the least, dug a hole in the ground and hid his master's money for safekeeping. He did not use what was entrusted to him; he received it in vain.

After a long time their master returned from his trip and called on them to give an account of what they had done. The master praised and rewarded the first two, who diligently worked with what had been entrusted to them. Then the servant who received the least, yet hid it, said, "Sir, I know you are a hard man, expecting something for nothing, so I was afraid and hid your money in the earth. Here it is" (author's paraphrase). The master replied, "You wicked and lazy servant!" (Matt. 25:26 NLT).

He says "servant." He does not use the word *heathen, stranger, foreigner,* or *enemy.* Those who have not received His grace are enemies (Rom. 5:10). Those who have not been saved are strangers or foreigners (Eph. 2:19). Those who do not believe in God are heathen. This man was not referred to as any of these, but rather as the master's servant. Jesus then made this point to all: "To those who use well what they are given, even more will be given, and they will have an abundance. But from those who are unfaithful, even what little they have will be taken away" (Matt. 25:29 NLT).

The master's judgment on all three servants dealt with how each used what he had been entrusted with. The judgment had nothing to do with whether or not they believed he existed. Of course the third servant believed in his master's existence, for he had received from him. He also knew his master would return, for he hid the money for safekeeping. However, he lived with an attitude that put off his master's return. He did not redeem the time; he had no righteous acts. The master pronounced this judgment on this lazy servant: "Now throw this useless servant into outer darkness, where there will be weeping and gnashing of teeth" (Matt. 25:30 NLT).

Though this parable develops in terms of investing money and not obtaining garments, the same principle applies: falling far short of obedient works. The judgment pronounced on the lazy servant correlates with the judgment of which Jesus warns the Laodicean church. They were naked because their works (not their belief in His existence) were lukewarm.

Jesus' next parable concerns the Last Judgment when He is going to judge all peoples. He will separate them as a shepherd separates the sheep from the goats.

> The King will say to [the sheep], "Come, you who are blessed by my Father, inherit the Kingdom prepared for you from the foundation of the world. For I was hungry, and you fed me. I was thirsty, and you gave me a drink. I was a stranger, and you invited me into your home. I was naked, and you gave me clothing. I was sick, and you cared for me. I was in prison, and you visited me." Then these righteous ones will reply, "Lord, when did we ever see you hungry and feed you? Or thirsty and give you something to drink? Or a stranger and show you hospitality? Or naked and give you clothing? When did we ever see you sick or in prison, and visit you?" And then the King will tell them, "I assure you, when you did it to one of the least of these my brothers and sisters, you were doing it to me!" (Matt. 25:34–40 NLT)

Jesus is addressing not only the physically sick, hungry, or imprisoned. He is speaking of the spiritually weak as well. In the greatest portion of His ministry, Jesus took care of spiritually poor people. He gave food to the spiritually hungry (Matt. 5:6). He gave drink to the spiritually thirsty (John 4:10). To those who are sick and in prison, Jesus says,

> The Spirit of the Lord is on me,
> because he has anointed me
> to preach good news to the poor.
> He has sent me to proclaim freedom for the prisoners
> and recovery of sight for the blind,
> to release the oppressed. (Luke 4:18 NIV)

If He referred only to physical works in the parable, then the twelve apostles would not have said to the church, "We apostles should spend our time preaching and teaching the word of God, not administering a food program" (Acts 6:2 NLT). This is not in any way meant to underestimate the importance of taking care of the physically poor or weak; both are important.

The key point is doing the works of Jesus. Jesus is our Teacher and Lord, yet He did not come to be served or to live His life in pleasure. He came to serve and to give His life as a ransom for many (Matt. 20:28)! The righteous saints rewarded in the parable were those who gave their lives to serve in Jesus' stead. Their works were hot, not lukewarm.

> Then the King will turn to those on the left and say, "Away with you, you cursed ones, into the eternal fire prepared for the Devil and his demons! For I was hungry, and you didn't feed me. I was thirsty, and you didn't give me anything to drink. I was a stranger, and you didn't invite me into your home. I was naked, and you gave me no clothing. I was sick and in prison, and you didn't visit me." Then

they will reply, "Lord, when did we ever see you hungry or thirsty or a stranger or naked or sick or in prison, and not help you?" And he will answer, "I assure you, when you refused to help the least of these my brothers and sisters, you were refusing to help me." And they will go away into eternal punishment, but the righteous will go into eternal life. (Matt. 25:41–46 NLT)

In this parable, the only difference between the two groups is what they did and did not do. In other words, the only difference was their works. The ones who were rewarded acted on the grace that was given to them and brought forth righteous acts. The people who were judged were made up of two segments, those who were heathen and those who were servants, but did nothing with the grace they had received. They did not produce righteous acts; they received the grace of God in vain.

Occasionally, I ask questions in large congregations in America and receive heartbreaking responses. For example, I request all the single moms to stand—and there are many—and ask them, "How often have people in the church come to you after a Sunday service and issued this invitation: 'Would you and your children come to our home today for a meal? We know your children don't have a father and need to see a godly example of one.'" The most positive responses have been two in a congregation of almost a thousand people.

I continue, "If your washing machine or another needed piece of equipment breaks down, you call one of the families of this church and ask for help, and that day brothers offer to help you, right?" They look at me, bewildered, some with tears in their eyes because I touch on the pressures affecting their lives. Again, no positive response. Other basic care questions have the same response.

I emphasize to the people that such care is not the responsibility of their pastors. Their responsibility is "to prepare God's people for works of service, so that the body of Christ may be built up" (Eph. 4:12 NIV).

I then change subjects and ask all the congregation: "How many of you minister with the prison outreach of the church?" Five to eight people may respond out of a large congregation. When I ask, "How many of you visit the hospitals and nursing homes?" I receive the same response. When I ask, "How many of you go out with the street teams to bring people the Word of God?" I receive the same response. The reason for such a low response is that 80 percent of most congregations live their lives basically for themselves and their immediate families. But unbelievers do that!

On the other hand, almost all of the ones who did not respond would attend a miracle service or the service of a "prophet" who will tell them they are going to have success in business or a glamorous ministry. They will drive miles for a double-portion anointing service or a renewal meeting. Why? Most likely not to serve Jesus more effectively, but to learn about benefits for themselves.

Recently I watched a popular television evangelist teaching a huge crowd on the anointing. He shared its price as the people listened intently. It was not hard to detect their passion for the power of God. Some even stood and stared at him with fire in their eyes. However, I sensed a grieving in my spirit, which was confirmed when a man placed a check in the hands of the evangelist. It was an "offering." I thought of Peter, when he was offered a financial gift for the anointing in the book of Acts. I was relieved to see the evangelist return the check to the man.

I immediately went to a remote place to pray. "Lord," I questioned, "I sensed a grieving. I think I know why, but I want You to explain it to me."

His still, small voice spoke in my heart, "John, they're passionate for My power, but for the wrong reasons. Power can make people feel significant. It gives them authority, it validates them, or it brings them wealth. They desire it not to serve, but to be successful."

The words of Jesus to the multitude before Him on Judgment Day flashed in my mind. They professed His lordship, validated by the fact that they had done miracles, cast out demons, and prophesied in His name. He turned to them and said, "Depart from Me, you who did not do the will of My Father!" (Matt. 7:21–23, author's paraphrase).

The Lord continued, "John, they didn't say, 'Lord, Lord, we visited those in prison in Your name, and we fed the hungry and clothed the naked in Your name.'"

Sobered, I agreed, "No, they didn't."

From this I could see two groups of people, which make up a large portion of the church. One group, the larger of the two, comes to church, but the people live their lives pursuing success in the world. The other group comes to church pursuing success in the ministry. A much smaller group is made up of those who passionately burn to please Jesus by serving His people and reaching the lost out of pure hearts!

Oh people, can you see the dangerous ways of our Western church? When many attend our churches, hear a sermon once or twice a week, then go out and live for themselves the rest of the week, what kind of garments do they have? Just about the only way to draw these "believers" to a service, other than usual times, is to entice them with a blessing that will benefit them in a selfish way. They expend their best energy and effort to pursue their own reward and gain. Most know the right things to say and appear kindhearted, yet they are not living for the Master. What will they do on Judgment Day when they are called upon to give an account of the grace that has been given them? Will they be naked, or will they be clothed with righteous (pure) acts?

Paul cries out:

> Therefore we make it our aim, whether present or absent, to be well pleasing to Him. For we must all appear before the judgment seat of Christ, that each one may receive the things done in the body, according to what he has done, whether good or bad. Knowing, therefore, the terror of the Lord, we persuade men. (2 Cor. 5:9–11 NKJV)

Have we considered the terror of the Lord? Do we mock His holiness by our trivial views of His judgment? Have we trusted in unsound and empty words? This leads us to the third thing Jesus tells the lukewarm to purchase from Him.

OINTMENT FOR THE EYES

After counseling the church to buy refined gold and white garments, Jesus advised them to buy from Him ointment for their eyes so that they might see. The ointment was eye salve, composed of various compounds and applied to the eyelids for medicinal purposes. The medical school at Laodicea was famous for it.

Since the people of the city were familiar with eye salve, Jesus used it to drive home the point that the church needed healing for spiritual blindness. Though it was a historic church, it has prophetic application. Many scholars believe it applies especially to the time period just before His return, which is our day. The church claims to see, but Jesus recognizes the reality and says, you "do not know that you are wretched, miserable, poor, blind, and naked."

Paul writes to believers, "I pray that the eyes of your heart may be enlightened" (Eph. 1:18 NASB). To be enlightened is to see clearly. We must see or perceive the way Jesus does. We can do this only by spending time in His presence, hearing His Word, and serving Him.

This general principle applies with natural leaders. You will learn a leader's perceptions by serving and spending time with him. My wife has spent more time with me than any other person on our ministry staff. She is a godly woman; she has been delighted to be my wife and serve under my God-given authority. She is the hardest worker on my staff. There have been numerous incidents when staff members needed decisions in my absence, and she has been able to give accurate direction each time.

Moses spent more time in the presence of God than any other

person in his day: "Moses was 120 years old when he died, yet his eyesight was clear, and he was as strong as ever" (Deut. 34:7 NLT). He also delighted himself in serving God more than any other, and God called him "My faithful servant" (*see* Num. 12:7).

The people of Israel, on the other hand, were not passionate for God's presence; they desired only His blessings. They would serve Him only if they saw the benefit. Thus, they did not see things the way God saw them.

They were corrected repeatedly for inaccurate perceptions. The problem reached its height when their leaders went into the promised land. Upon returning, ten of the leaders told the congregation that "we seemed like grasshoppers in our own eyes, and we looked the same to them" (Num. 13:33 NIV).

Caleb and Joshua saw the situation differently. They reported to the people, "Do not rebel against the LORD. And do not be afraid of the people of the land, because we will swallow them up. Their protection is gone, but the LORD is with us. Do not be afraid of them" (Num. 14:9 NIV). Why were these men so different in the way they saw the situation? Joshua had a passion to spend time with God. Joshua went as close as he was permitted to the mountain (Ex. 24:13).

Later, before the tabernacle was erected, Moses set up a tent far from the camp and called it the tent of meeting. If anyone wanted to seek the Lord, he was instructed to go outside the camp to the tent of meeting. Other than Moses, we have no record of anyone going to the tent except Joshua. When Moses went to that place of meeting, all the people stood at the doors of their own tents and worshiped from afar. They respected the man for seeking God, yet they did not go near, for their hearts would be revealed. But Scripture records that when Moses returned to the camp, "his young aide Joshua son of Nun did not leave the tent" (Ex. 33:7–11 NIV).

Two things are evident here. First, Joshua had intense passion for God's presence. Joshua remained even after Moses left the meeting place. Second, Joshua was Moses' aide. He, too, was a faithful servant of the Lord; his works corresponded with his faith. Joshua's sight was clear because he spent time with God and brought forth righteous works of service.

Today, some people spend hours in their "prayer closets," but they do not serve. They are always fouling things up in their churches because of their blindness. They are hyperspiritual people who are not bringing forth true fruit in the kingdom. They are blind because they do not serve. It takes both spending time with the Lord and serving.

Just as Moses' sight was accurate, so was Joshua's. Both men spent time with God and were servants bringing forth righteous acts. The children of Israel saw themselves as grasshoppers, and they said the enemy saw them as grasshoppers. Joshua and Caleb reported that the enemies' protection and strength were gone. Who saw it accurately? Forty years later when Joshua sent two spies into the same land, one of the inhabitants reported to the spies,

> For we have heard how the LORD dried up the water of the Red Sea for you when you came out of Egypt . . . And as soon as we heard these things, our hearts melted; neither did there remain any more courage in anyone because of you, for the LORD your God, He is God in heaven above and on earth beneath. (Josh. 2:10–11 NKJV)

Joshua saw accurately, whereas the other leaders' perceptions were completely in error. This situation correlates with that of the lazy servant, who received the grace of his master in vain. By the time of his master's return, the servant saw him as a hard man, who expected something from nothing. His perception was totally inaccurate. More than likely, his erroneous perceptions grew stronger the longer he refrained from bringing forth the works the master asked of him.

As we discussed earlier, today there are two groups of people in the church whose sight is dim; they do not see the way Jesus sees. The first group included those who are not seeking God as they should. They respect the preacher who seeks God and brings forth a message from heaven. Yet they have not gone outside the camp to meet with Jesus. They have not heeded the exhortation, "Let us go forth to Him, outside the camp" (Heb. 13:13 NKJV). Their works are lukewarm.

The second group includes those who are seeking Jesus, yet not serving. They are seeking Him for what He can do for them. To put it bluntly, they are usually the ones who are bringing more headaches to godly pastors than anyone else! They have "religious" or "spiritual" behavior, but their works are lukewarm.

Oh, people of God, we don't need refreshing or renewal in the church. We need reformation! Renewal refreshes what we already have. Reformation calls for a complete change of the way we perceive and live. We have believed for too long in a counterfeit grace that has led the church into a lukewarm state. You can teach something that is inaccurate for so long that you eventually believe it is truth. Then when truth is spoken, you reject it, calling it extreme or error. Renewal or revival will only strengthen inaccurate perceptions. Our eyes need to be opened to see as He sees! As the psalmist says, "In Your light we see light" (Ps. 36:9 NKJV).

CHAPTER 12

AS MANY AS I LOVE . . .

If we are going to be like Jesus when He returns,
then one of us is going to have to change.

As we learned in the previous chapter, Jesus tells the church of Laodicea to buy from Him gold refined in fire, white garments, and ointment for their eyes. Then He says, "As many as I love, I rebuke and chasten" (Rev. 3:19 NKJV).

Out of His love He rebukes and chastens us. The writer of Hebrews expands on this point:

> My son, do not despise the chastening of the LORD,
> Nor be discouraged when you are rebuked by Him;
> For whom the LORD loves He chastens,
> And scourges every son whom He receives. (Heb. 12:5–6 NKJV)

To chasten means "to correct or discipline." To scourge means "to punish." In fact, the Greek word for "scourge" is *mastigoo*. This word is found only seven times in the New Testament. In all other places the word means to physically scourge with a whip. Our Father certainly does not use a scourging whip; however, His chastening can be severe. That is why the writer tells us not to despise it. At times in the midst of His correction, I felt as if I were going to die from the inward pain, but yielding to it always turned out for my good and ignited a fresh flame of holiness within my heart.

GOD'S CHILDREN

The most dedicated of God's children need correction. Though God may allow others to go on in their error or sin uncorrected, He will not allow that of His sons and daughters. Just as no wise and good father would overlook faults in his own children, as he may with others, so the Lord will not allow His children to continue in what would ruin them.

To be allowed to sin without a rebuke is an alarming sign of alienation from God. Scripture clearly states that those who do not experience His correction are illegitimate children, not true sons or daughters. They may call Him Father, but their claim to Him is spawned out of a counterfeit conversion.

I have preached strong messages from the heart of God and afterward heard two completely different responses. Many times one person received correction from the Father; the other was virtually unaffected because he was not a true child of God. One incident happened within a family. After I had preached a very sobering message on rebellion one Sunday morning, more than half of the congregation received the call to repentance at the close. The pastor and his wife took me to a member's home for lunch following the service. The woman of the house could not stop discussing how God had chastened her through His Word in the service. Her countenance gave evidence of her encounter with the Lord. The Holy Spirit had dealt strongly with her. But in the course of the conversation she said to me with a puzzled tone, "My daughter said to me after the service, 'That man was loud, and his message made no sense.'"

I perceived when I first entered the house that the daughter was not truly saved. Her mother's statement only confirmed what I discerned.

The mother, who loved the Lord deeply, was brought under discipline, as were the majority of the others in attendance that morning. Yet the daughter, who sat right next to her in the service, was unaffected—even though there was obviously insubordination in her life. The daughter's statements and behavior that afternoon affirmed that she was not a true child of God. However, if I had asked the daughter whether she was a Christian, she would have said, "Yes."

God chastens His own. His first desire is to speak to us in a stern manner through His Word, as in this woman's example. But if we are not listening, He will use hardship and affliction to bring correction. The psalmist declares,

> Before I was afflicted I went astray,
> But now I keep Your word . . .
> I know, O LORD, that Your judgments are right,
> And that in faithfulness You have afflicted me. (Ps. 119:67, 75 NKJV)

Paul says concerning the Father's discipline: "That is why many of you are weak and sick and some have even died. But if we examine ourselves, we will not be examined by God and judged in this way. But when we are judged and disciplined by the Lord, we will not be condemned with the world" (1 Cor. 11:30–32 NLT).

God prefers for us to heed His words of correction, but no matter how He corrects us, no method is pleasant at the time we receive it. The writer of Hebrews confirms, "Now no chastening seems to be joyful for the present, but painful" (12:11 NKJV). God is much more concerned about our condition than our comfort. The writer notes that God corrects us for "our profit, that we may be partakers of His holiness" (12:10 NKJV). The work of holiness is the purpose of His correction.

The writer continues, "Therefore strengthen the hands which hang down, and the feeble knees, and make straight paths for your feet, so that what is lame may not be dislocated, but rather be healed" (Heb. 12:12–13 NKJV). Hands speak of service, or the works we bring forth in the Lord. Knees refer to our walk, or the manner in which we live. To strengthen is not to flatter; it is to speak the truth in love. Jesus was not weakening the church of Laodicea with His stern words of warning and correction. He was giving them what would rekindle their fire. He was bringing correction so that they might be partakers of His holiness. Of course, that would occur only if they received His correction.

Why have we withdrawn from strengthening the weak in the church? Why have we not spoken messages in the same manner as Jesus? Why are the majority of the messages spoken and written in our Western churches about peace, prosperity, and happiness, when we desperately need to be confronted with truth? God says through Jeremiah about the preachers of his day, who were soft-pedaling messages to a lukewarm people,

> If they had stood in My counsel,
> And had caused My people to hear My words,
> Then they would have turned them from their evil way
> And from the evil of their doings. (Jer. 23:22 NKJV)

Are we directing and turning hearts toward righteousness to prepare our generation to face a holy God, or are we tickling ears with words that do not call for godly change?

PEACEMAKING OR PEACEKEEPING?

We read on in Hebrews, "Pursue peace with all people, and holiness, without which no one will see the Lord: looking carefully lest anyone fall short of the grace of God" (Heb. 12:14–15 NKJV). The first thing the writer declares is to pursue peace with all.

Jesus never said, "Blessed are the peacekeepers"; He said, "Blessed are the peacemakers" (Matt. 5:9 NKJV).

You may ask, "Is there a difference?"

Absolutely! A peacekeeper maintains peace at all costs. Thus, he will compromise truth to avoid confrontation. A peacekeeper, therefore, will not bring the words from the heart of God that call for a change when they are needed, such as Jesus did with the majority of the churches in Revelation. Then people remain comfortable in their present state when they need godly change.

A peacemaker, on the other hand, seeks true peace, and if need be, he tenaciously confronts with truth or righteousness to bring forth real peace. A peacemaker loves righteousness and hates sin. He does not back off. He calls sin just what it is: sin, not a mistake or weakness. His hatred for sin grows out of his love for God and for people. His true desire is to see what is best for people, not necessarily what makes them happy. He is more concerned with bringing them what will help them rather than being popular or pleasing to them. He has no interest in his personal gain. He delights in true mercy and justice. He loves holiness; his heart burns for it, for his heart burns for God!

STRENGTHENING THE WEAK TO PURSUE HOLINESS

The writer urges readers to pursue holiness, "without which no one will see the Lord." Earlier we learned that the children of Israel confessed a desire to draw near to God that truly did not exist. It was their intention, not their real desire. They could not draw near to God, as Moses did, because they did not remove the desires that Egypt imparted to them. Drawing near to God would have revealed their impurity, which they did not want confronted.

The writer of Hebrews illuminates what God has been saying to His people throughout the ages. Isaiah similarly writes, "Strengthen the weak hands, and make firm the feeble knees" (Isa. 35:3 NKJV).

After the hands and knees are strengthened, the Old Testament prophet announces that the eyes of the blind will be opened and the ears of the deaf will be unclogged. The wilderness will turn into a fruitful land, all because His people were strengthened to walk in holiness! Isaiah states,

> And a highway will be there, a roadway,
> And it will be called the Highway of Holiness.
> The unclean will not travel on it,
> But it will be for him who walks that way,
> And fools will not wander on it. (Isa. 35:8 NASB)

God's ways are higher than man's ways. This highway of holiness speaks of the path of life, which Jesus explains is narrow (Matt. 7:13–14). It speaks of the higher walk of holiness. We attain this higher walk of holiness only when we are open to and receive His correction.

According to the prophet, fools will not wander on it. A fool is one who sees his own thoughts and life as the measure of wisdom. Proverbs 12:15 (NKJV) points out that "the way of a fool is right in his own eyes." And again we learn from Proverbs that a fool is "self-confident" (14:16 NKJV). And Proverbs 18:2 (NKJV) declares that "a fool has no delight in understanding, but in expressing his own heart." A fool, therefore, is deceived. Proverbs 14:8 (NKJV) tells us that "the folly of fools is deceit."

The members of the Laodicean church were deceived. They believed they were blessed and prosperous. Yet they lacked the true riches of life: character, godly works, and the ability to see as Jesus sees. Jesus' words of rebuke, warning, and correction, though very tough, were to deliver them from the path of foolishness and to direct them to the path of holiness. He was strengthening their weak hands and firming up their feeble knees.

THE PATH TO MOUNT ZION

Those today who will not heed correction will miss the only path leading to His glory. Holiness does not come easily. There is the correction of refining, purging, and cleansing—all of which are of no effect without repentance. For this reason Jesus says to the Laodicean church: "Therefore be zealous and repent" (Rev. 3:19 NKJV).

True repentance is a change of mind and attitude toward sin and its causes, not merely toward the consequences of sin. We have learned to sorrow over the consequences of sin without forsaking its nature. To be zealous, as Jesus commands this church, is to desire passionately to change from where we presently are to His glorious nature. Let's face it, if we are going to be like Jesus when He returns (1 John 3:2), then one of us is going to have to change, and it is not going to be Him! Only His training and correction will conform us into His image.

Isaiah indicates that those who do not remain foolish, by receiving God's correction, will be called the ransomed of the Lord and they will "return, and come to Zion with singing, with everlasting joy on their heads" (Isa. 35:10 NKJV). The reference here to Zion is important.

The writer of Hebrews draws a vivid picture: "You have not come to a mountain that can be touched and that is burning with fire; to darkness, gloom and storm; to a trumpet blast or to such a voice speaking words that those who heard it begged that no further word be spoken to them" (Heb. 12:18–19 NIV). The mountain is the one we discussed in the earlier chapters of this book. Again we hear the sad testimony that the people begged God to stop speaking. They rejected His chastening for it exposed their hearts. They were foolish!

Zephaniah 3:2 (NKJV) declares of Israel,

> She has not obeyed His voice,
> She has not received correction;
> She has not trusted in the LORD,
> She has not drawn near to her God.

God laments by saying, "In vain I have chastened your children; they received no correction" (Jer. 2:30 NKJV). If they had pursued holiness by being willing to be corrected and repenting of their ways, then they could have drawn near to God on the mountain.

Now we are faced with a similar opportunity, although we have not come to a mountain that we can see and touch. We have come to a different mountain, the one to which Isaiah refers:

> But you have come to Mount Zion and to the city of the living God. (Heb. 12:22 NKJV)

He is still on a mountain, yet it is not a physical one called Sinai. It is a more real and enduring mountain, called Zion. The only path to this mountain is the highway of holiness! Moses walked on this path; he forsook Egypt in his heart and readily received God's words, which included correction. The children of Israel begged God not to speak, for they did not desire His word, which would expose their hearts, to bring correction. In the light of their actions we are admonished:

> See that you do not refuse [God] who speaks. For if they did not escape who refused [God] who spoke on earth, much more shall we not escape if we turn away from [God] who speaks from heaven. (Heb. 12:25 NKJV)

God spoke on the earth from Sinai; He speaks today from His heavenly mountain called Zion. What sobering words of warning we hear in this statement! If the children of Israel did not escape when God spoke His word from Sinai, which would have brought training and correction to them, much more shall we not escape if we fail to heed His words that He speaks from Mount Zion, which will bring training and correction.

The children of Israel did not want to hear His words from the midst of His glory because they would have exposed their polluted hearts, so they had to draw back. Yet, later, when Moses was on the mountain, they formed a Jehovah that would speak to them through their prophets what they wanted to hear—smooth things that would tickle their ears and give them what their carnal appetites desired. All the while on the mountain's summit Moses was hearing the true word of the Lord that was transforming him. When he came down from the mountain, his face was lit with the radiance of God.

To Moses, God's word was transformation. To the children of Israel, His word shook the mountain and the ground they stood on, and, it shook them to the point of drawing back. The writer continues,

> Whose voice then shook the earth; but now He has promised, say-ing, "Yet once more I shake not only the earth, but also heaven." Now this, "Yet once more," indicates the removal of those things that are being shaken, as of things that are made, that the things which cannot be shaken may remain. (Heb. 12:26–27 NKJV)

Jesus' words of correction shook the Laodicean church. They were comfortable in their Christianity, all seemed well, yet the true word of the Lord shook their foundations. God will once again shake His church, then the nations. Shaking removes what is not built on a proper foundation. It removes what is dead or not good. It purges so that what is living or pure may remain. The only ones who need to fear God's shaking are those who do not fear Him.

Isaiah speaks to this issue:

> The sinners in Zion are afraid;
> Fearfulness has seized the hypocrites:
> "Who among us shall dwell with the devouring fire?
> Who among us shall dwell with everlasting burnings?"
> He who walks righteously and speaks uprightly,
> He who despises the gain of oppressions,
> Who gestures with his hands, refusing bribes,

Who stops his ears from hearing of bloodshed,
And shuts his eyes from seeing evil:
He will dwell on high;
His place of defense will be the fortress of rocks;
Bread will be given him,
His water will be sure. (Isa. 33:14–16 NKJV)

He does not say "the sinners in Egypt" but rather "the sinners in Zion." He is referring to those in the church who lack the fear of the Lord and are not pursuing holiness. They are not secure, and they will be shaken. And fearfulness will not seize them until God reveals His glory! The devouring fire or everlasting burnings refer to God.

The writer of Hebrews finishes the chapter: "Therefore, since we are receiving a kingdom which cannot be shaken, let us have grace, by which we may serve God acceptably with reverence and godly fear. For our God is a consuming fire" (Heb. 12:28–29 NKJV). Our God is a consuming fire! Although many Old Testament passages have been cited in this book, I have, by the grace of God, attempted to rightly divide the Word of God by bringing them forth in the light of New Testament writings. Our God is love, but He is also a consuming fire.

That description of His glorious presence is not something to be taken as lightly as too many of us have done. To confirm His awesome glory, the writer of Hebrews remarks, "The sight was so terrifying that Moses said, 'I am trembling with fear'" (Heb. 12:21 NIV). This response corresponds with the apostle John's testimony of seeing Jesus: "And when I saw Him, I fell at His feet as dead" (Rev. 1:17 NKJV).

THAT WE MAY BE HOLY

Yes, He loves us with a greater love than the mind can comprehend. But that love in no way diminishes His holiness. That is why the writer of Hebrews tells us, "Let us have grace, by which we may serve God acceptably with reverence and godly fear." Oh, how we need His grace to walk in the fear of the Lord, that we may be holy, as He is holy (Lev. 19:2; Matt. 5:48: 1 Peter 1:16)!

As we have learned, only those who fear God and pursue holiness will be able to dwell in His glorious presence. To return to the Scripture passage we quoted from in the second chapter of this book:

For you are the temple of the living God. As God has said:

"I will dwell in them
And walk among them.
I will be their God,
And they shall be My people."
Therefore
"Come out from among them
And be separate, says the Lord.
Do not touch what is unclean,
And I will receive you.
I will be a Father to you,
And you shall be My sons and daughters,
Says the LORD Almighty."

Therefore, having these promises, beloved, let us cleanse ourselves from all filthiness of the flesh and spirit, perfecting holiness in the fear of God. (2 Cor. 6:16–7:1 NKJV)

Now you have heard the background. You have not walked into this true drama right at the punch line, missing its context. I hope that the background has become clear to you. Your heart will burn with passion if you desire His glory more than you desire anything else.

CHAPTER 13

HOLY FIRE WITHIN

We are called to burn with the fire of His glory, as Moses, Isaiah,
Jeremiah, John, Paul, and others were.

All of God's people have required in one form or another His correction, from the holy prophets of old to the apostles of the New
Testament. The same is certainly true today. The key, though, is
what we will do with it. Pride keeps us from receiving God's chastening; thus, we forfeit the benefit of the work of His holiness. But
if we humble ourselves and accept His chastening, we are enabled
to hear His voice with greater accuracy and see with greater clarity,
positioning ourselves to mature in our relationship with Him.
Habakkuk writes,

> I will stand my watch
> And set myself on the rampart,
> And watch to see what He will say to me,
> And what I will answer when I am corrected. (Hab. 2:1 NKJV)

This man actually positioned himself to receive God's correction,
knowing it would yield a keener insight to God's heart and ways.
Then he would be a more effective servant.

In the Year King Uzziah Died

Isaiah, too, kept himself in a ready position to accept what the Lord would say to him. He records, "In the year that King Uzziah died, I saw the Lord sitting on a throne, high and lifted up, and the train of His robe filled the temple" (Isa. 6:1 NKJV).

A few years ago while I was in prayer concerning this portion of Scripture, the Lord spoke to me. I was meditating on the fact that Isaiah saw the Lord in His glory. I thought, *The church needs to see a fresh vision of Jesus in His glory.*

Then I heard the Lord say, "That is not how I started the verse." Puzzled, I returned to my Bible to read, "In the year that King Uzziah died." The Lord stopped me and said, "King Uzziah had to die before Isaiah had a fresh vision of Me!" He continued, "Before the church can have a fresh vision of Me, Uzziah must die!"

I thought, *Who is this guy Uzziah, and what does he have to do with seeing Jesus?* I turned to a concordance, found all the references to him, read the accounts of his life, and in them discovered a significant revelation.

Uzziah was a descendant of King David. He was crowned king at the age of sixteen. At first he sought God diligently. You would, too, if you were made ruler of a nation at sixteen. More than likely, he was overwhelmed and humbled by the magnitude of the undertaking. It is recorded, "As long as he sought the LORD, God made him prosper" (2 Chron. 26:5 NKJV).

Because he utterly relied on God, Uzziah was greatly blessed. He made war against the Philistines, defeating them in numerous cities, as well as the Arabians, Meunites, and Ammonites. The nation became strong both economically and militarily. The people prospered under his leadership.

His success was the result of the grace of God on his life. But something changed. His overconfidence replaced his humility: "But when he was strong his heart was lifted up, to his destruction, for he transgressed against the LORD his God by entering the temple of the LORD to burn incense on the altar of incense" (2 Chron. 26:16 NKJV).

It was not in a weak moment, but when Uzziah was strong, that his heart was lifted in pride. As he surveyed the prosperity and success that encompassed all his domain, his heart ceased to seek the Lord. He could do it on his own; he knew how. His achievements mounted, so he assumed God would bless all he undertook; before, he was blessed because he humbly sought God.

This did not happen overnight, and it can easily happen to anyone. God warned me, "John, most in the kingdom who have fallen have done so not in the dry times, but in the abundant times." Why? Because when we achieve great accomplishments, it becomes easier to lose sight of the fact that He has given us everything.

Many people have fallen into this pattern. When they are first saved, they hunger to know the Lord and His ways. Their humility is evident because they seek Him and trust Him for everything. They arrive at church with a hunger in their hearts. "Lord, I want to know You!" They submit to God's direct and delegated authority. In true humility they readily receive His correction, no matter how or through whom He brings it. But they reach a point where they have amassed knowledge and waxed strong through experience and accomplishment and their attitude changes. Instead of reading the Bible with the intent of asking, "Lord, reveal Yourself and Your ways to me," they use it to support their established doctrine and read what they believe. No longer do they listen for God's heavenly voice in the voice of their pastor; they lean back with folded arms and an attitude of, "Let's see what he knows." They are experts in Scriptures but have forfeited their tenderness and humility of heart. The grace to serve God wanes, as pride displaces it (see James 4:6).

This problem seems to happen too easily in the church of America since there is so much teaching available to us. We read in 1 Corinthians 8:1 (NKJV): "We know that we all have knowledge.

Knowledge puffs up [pride], but love edifies." Love does not seek its own but lays its life down for the Master and those it is called to serve. Pride seeks its own behind a mask of religion. God explained that knowledge gained without love results in pride.

Let's ask an important question about King Uzziah. When pride entered his heart, did he become more or less religious? The amazing answer is that he became more religious! His heart was lifted up, and he entered the temple to worship. Pride and a religious spirit go hand in hand. A religious spirit causes a person to think he is humble through his appearance of "false spirituality," and the truth is, he is proud. On the other hand, pride keeps a person in bondage to a religious spirit because he is too proud to admit he has one! Pride is well camouflaged in the church, for it hides behind a religious, charismatic, evangelical, or pentecostal mask.

Uzziah was then confronted with truth:

> Azariah the priest with eighty other courageous priests of the LORD followed him in. They confronted him and said, "It is not right for you, Uzziah, to burn incense to the LORD. That is for the priests, the descendants of Aaron, who have been consecrated to burn incense. Leave the sanctuary, for you have been unfaithful; and you will not be honored by the LORD God." (2 Chron. 26:17–18 NIV)

God had brought His correction through those valiant men, and Uzziah's response was certainly not godly: "Then Uzziah became furious; and he had a censer in his hand to burn incense. And while he was angry with the priests, leprosy broke out on his forehead, before the priests in the house of the LORD, beside the incense altar" (2 Chron. 26:19 NKJV).

Uzziah became angry. Pride will always justify itself. This self-defense will be coupled with anger. A proud person blames everyone else while excusing himself. Uzziah directed his anger at the priests, but the problem lay deep within himself. Pride had blinded his eyes! Instead of humbling himself to receive God's correction through those men, he allowed anger to fuel his pride. Leprosy broke out on his forehead where all could see it. Leprosy in his case was an outward manifestation of an inward condition, and its source was pride.

The same is true today. Leprosy in the Old Testament is a type of sin in the New Testament. Many times outward sin is nothing more than a manifestation of the pride from within, which blinds and keeps a person from receiving God's correction.

After hearing what God spoke to my heart and then reviewing Uzziah's life, I realized pride blinds us from seeing Jesus. We must see Him, for Scripture declares as we behold Him, we are changed into His image: "We all, with unveiled face, beholding as in a mirror the glory of the Lord, are being transformed into the same image from glory to glory, just as by the Spirit of the Lord" (2 Cor. 3:18 NKJV).

We must behold Him so that we may be conformed to His image, thus giving us the ability to see as He sees. Pride will keep us from beholding Him afresh, thus blinding us and moving us into the dangerous arena of deception. The people in the Laodicean church were kept from seeing Jesus because of their pride. They believed they were spiritual, but His rebuke showed otherwise. They were stagnant, without His transforming power. They had a form of Christianity, but lacked the corresponding works of Jesus.

HOLY, HOLY, HOLY!

Isaiah saw the Lord in His glory. We know it had to have been a spiritual vision, for no man in a fleshly body can see God's face and live. When Isaiah saw His throne, he could not help noticing the massive angels, which are referred to as seraphim. He wrote that each had six wings, with two of the six covering the face. And one cried to another:

"Holy, holy, holy is the LORD of hosts;
The whole earth is full of His glory!"
And the posts of the door were shaken by the voice of him who cried
out, and the house was filled with smoke. (Isa. 6:3–4 NKJV)

The angels were not singing a hymn. There is a song taken from this verse, but often people sing it in a monotone voice. No, the angelic beings were responding to what they saw, even with their faces covered. Every moment another facet of His glory was being revealed, and they cried out, "Holy!" They shouted it so loudly that they shook the architecture of heaven! It's hard enough to shake earth's structures with noise, let alone heaven's. The angels were not singing a song, thinking, *I have been near His throne for trillions of years. I would like to get a break and explore other parts of heaven.* No, they didn't want to be anywhere else because the Creator is much more beautiful and wonderful than His creation. The psalmist cried out that he would rather be a doorkeeper in the throne room of God than be in lush palaces where His presence did not abide (Ps. 84).

Why did the angels cry out, "Holy, holy, holy"? Why three times? The usage represents a literary style found in Hebrew forms of writing. The repetition is a form of emphasis. When we want to emphasize the importance of a word or phrase in English, we have several methods. We can boldface it, italicize it, underline it, use all capitals, or add an exclamation point.

A Jewish writer could indicate emphasis by repeating a word. Usually, the word is repeated twice; for example, Jesus says, "Not everyone who says to Me, 'Lord, Lord,' shall enter the kingdom of heaven" (Matt. 7:21 NKJV). Jesus did not actually say "Lord" twice; rather, He put an emphasis on the word "Lord" that the writer wanted to capture.

Only a few references in the Scriptures repeat a word three times. One occasion occurs when the angel pronounced judgment on the inhabitants of the earth in the book of Revelation; the angel cried out, "Woe, woe, woe" (Rev. 8:13 NKJV). The message issued with the repetition is that the judgments that have already happened have been hard, but what is coming is beyond comprehension.

However, only once in the Scriptures is an attribute of God mentioned three times in succession. These angels were not crying out, "Power, power, power!" Nor did they shout, "Love, love, love!" or "Faithful, faithful, faithful!" Yes, God is powerful, God is love, and God is faithful, but the characteristic that stands above all others is His holiness. In that holiness is found the brightness of His being or the fire of God!

WOE IS ME

Once Isaiah saw Him, he did not say, "Wow, there He is!" Rather he cried out:

> Woe is me, for I am undone!
> Because I am a man of unclean lips,
> And I dwell in the midst of a people of unclean lips;
> For my eyes have seen the King,
> The LORD of hosts. (Isa. 6:5 NKJV)

The word *woe* has lost its strength in our language today. It is the word used to pronounce the greatest form of God's judgment. As already stated, when the angels pronounced woe on the inhabitants of the earth, the angel was actually saying, "The most severe judgment is about to fall on you." Jesus used this word concerning Judas. The word is so severe that Jesus said, "It would have been good for that man if he had never been born" (Mark 14:21 NKJV). It was rare for a prophet to pronounce the word *woe* on a person's life. What was even more astounding was for a godly man, Isaiah, to pronounce it upon himself!

Immediately following his pronouncement of judgment on himself, Isaiah cried out, "I am undone!" To be undone means to be coming apart at the seams. Isaiah stood before a holy God. For the first time in his life, he really grasped who God was, and for the first time in his life, he really understood who he was.

In that single moment all self-esteem was shattered. All confidence in himself and humanity was annihilated. Never again would psychiatry be an issue in relating to life. If there was any pride, it was no more to be found. Isaiah was prostrate on his face, groveling on the floor of the throne room. Every fiber of his being was trembling and exposed. He looked for a place to hide but could find none. He saw more than ever before his desperate need of mercy and grace in order to survive, let alone stand before such a holy God, who is Lord of all!

CLEANSING, SERVICE, CLARITY OF VISION

When he felt as if he couldn't stand another moment, he described what happened next:

> Then one of the seraphim flew to me, having in his hand a live coal which he had taken with the tongs from the altar. And he touched my mouth with it, and said:
>
> > "Behold, this has touched your lips;
> > Your iniquity is taken away,
> > And your sin purged." (Isa. 6:6–7 NKJV)

God gives mercy and grace to the humble. The burning coal purged or refined Isaiah. After he was purified, he heard the voice of God say, "Whom shall I send, and who will go for Us?" (Isa. 6:8 NKJV).

Because he was purged, he could hear the voice of God more clearly: "Who will go for Us?" In other words, "Who will bring forth pure works of righteousness?" Isaiah immediately responded, "Here am I! Send me" (Isa. 6:8 NKJV).

Isaiah heard the words of God's heart:

> Go, and tell this people [who were His people],
> "Keep on hearing, but do not understand;
> Keep on seeing, but do not perceive." (Isa. 6:9–10 NKJV)

Included in the people who God said were blind and deaf were known prophets and teachers of the Scriptures. They were not speaking what He was saying because they could not hear clearly.

God is speaking, but are people really hearing? These verses remind me of a conversation with a very godly friend of mine. (Earlier I wrote about him as the man who discipled me in college.) I had traveled into his area, and he picked me up at the airport. He had been meditating and praying for hours before my arrival. He said to me in tears, "John, God has so much to say to America, but He can't find the people to say it." My heart burned with passion at his words; I knew I was far from where I was to be as one of the Lord's ambassadors. I immediately thought of Isaiah. Once he was refined or purified, God's voice became clear and he was able to speak God's heart, not just principles. I thought, *It's not that there aren't people who can speak the principles of truth from Scripture in America. The real issue is, Are there men and women who will separate and humble themselves in order for God's purifying work to be accomplished, so they can accurately hear God's heart to proclaim it?*

DINING WITH JESUS

Let's return to the church of Laodicea, which represents us prophetically. Jesus sternly corrects the church, then gives the charge, "Therefore be zealous and repent." It is up to these people. Or should I say us? Will we heed His correction, or will we be foolish as the children of Israel were?

Jesus continues, "Behold, I stand at the door and knock. If anyone hears My voice and opens the door, I will come in to him and dine with him, and he with Me" (Rev. 3:20 NKJV). Oh, hear His words to His church of the last days! He says to His people who are preaching and teaching, "If anyone hears My voice." Doesn't that break your heart? Have we been so impure in our relationship with Him, due to our love for pleasure and personal gain, that we have not heard His heart? Have we been so entangled in the world's manners and desires that we have become a people who say we hear His voice, when in actuality we have been far from His heart cry?

If you'll recall, Jesus told the church to buy from Him refined gold, white garments, which represented righteous acts, and ointment in order to see as He sees. This pattern is evident in Isaiah's testimony. When he humbled himself to receive God's correction, he was refined. After that he was passionate to do righteous or holy works. Next, he cried out that the people were not seeing correctly; they were blind! They needed ointment. God had removed the veil from Isaiah's eyes through his humility, God's correction and purging, and Isaiah's willingness to bring forth righteous works.

Listen again to Jesus: "If anyone hears My voice and opens the door, I will come in to him and dine with him, and he with Me." This saying has a double application. Yes, this is the church just prior to the Second Coming, and therefore, it refers to the Second Coming. Luke records similar words of Jesus:

> Be dressed ready for service and keep your lamps burning, like men waiting for their master to return from a wedding banquet, so that when he comes and knocks they can immediately open the door for him. It will be good for those servants whose master finds them watching when he comes. I tell you the truth, he will dress himself to serve, will have them recline at the table and will come and wait on them. (Luke 12:35–37 NIV)

Our Master will wait on us, even though we should forever wait on Him. He is a servant in the truest sense. He owes no debt to us, as we do to Him, yet He desires to serve His faithful ones. He will serve us at the marriage supper of the Lamb.

There is a second application. When Jesus says, "I will come in to him and dine with him, and he with Me," He is speaking not just of the marriage supper, but of giving us the true manna, which is the revelation of Himself. He declares, "I am the living bread which came down from heaven" (John 6:51 NKJV). He is the living Word of God, which we live on (Deut. 8:2–3).

Jeremiah puts it this way:

> Your words were found, and I ate them,
> And Your word was to me the joy and rejoicing of my heart.
> (Jer. 15:16 NKJV)

Jeremiah was another, like Isaiah, who had undergone God's purification. And, like Moses, he had no desire for the world's system. He had separated himself in order to know God. His delight was the word of God; it was his food. Because he preached the heart of God to a people who were backslidden, he was persecuted:

> So the word of the LORD has brought me
>   insult and reproach all day long.
> But if I say, "I will not mention him
>   or speak any more in his name,"
> his word is in my heart like a fire,
>   a fire shut up in my bones.
> I am weary of holding it in;
>   indeed, I cannot. (Jer. 20:8–9 NIV)

John the Baptist was another who hungered for the word of God. He had separated himself from the world and religious hypocrisy.

His heritage was to be trained in Jerusalem with other priests' sons to be a leader. He forsook what man planned for him and obeyed God. In the desert, the word of the Lord came to him. He, too, brought forth the heart of God. Jesus said of him: "He was the burning and shining lamp, and you were willing for a time to rejoice in his light" (John 5:35 NKJV).

We are called to burn with the fire of His glory, as Moses, Isaiah, Jeremiah, John, Paul, and others were. But it will never happen if we do not separate ourselves from the desires of this world. We are called to live as pilgrims and strangers to this world. Our true satisfaction will come only when we are so consumed by His Word that it is our meditation all day. Then the fire of God will burn brightly in and upon us. When young men and women fall in love, no one has to tell them, "Think about your loved one all day long." No, in every free moment they think about the loved one.

Malachi foresaw two kinds of people in the church in the last days. Both will go through the refining process we have learned about in earlier chapters. The first will complain, saying, "What profit is it that we are serving God, for the wicked have more fun than we do? We serve God and keep going through trials and tribulations" (Mal. 3:14–15, author's paraphrase).

The report of the second group of people is different:

> Then those who feared the LORD spoke to one another,
> And the LORD listened and heard them;
> So a book of remembrance was written before Him
> For those who fear the LORD
> And who meditate on His name. (Mal. 3:16 NKJV)

They love His Word and ways more than any suffering can overshadow. But the prophet speaks of what will happen:

> "For behold, the day is coming,
> Burning like an oven,

And all the proud, yes, all who do wickedly will be stubble.
And the day which is coming shall burn them up,"
Says the LORD of hosts,
"That will leave them neither root nor branch.
But to you who fear My name
The Sun of Righteousness shall arise
With healing in His wings;
And you shall go out
And grow fat like stall-fed calves.
You shall trample the wicked,
For they shall be ashes under the soles of your feet
On the day that I do this,"
Says the LORD of hosts. (Mal. 4:1–3 NKJV)

He speaks not of the "Son of Righteousness," but of the "Sun of Righteousness." The sun is a massive ball of fire. That is how Jesus is going to manifest Himself in the last days to those who fear Him. They will have meditated on His Word out of their pure love for His ways. The fire of His glory will arise upon them and will be seen by people in gross darkness. As never before, a harvest of souls will come forth as a result of the ministries of these burning and shining lamps. Their hearts will be ablaze with His Word, and no darkness will overcome them.

We see a glimpse of this with two of Jesus' disciples after the Resurrection:

Now behold, two of them were traveling that same day to a village called Emmaus, which was seven miles from Jerusalem. And they talked together of all these things which had happened. So it was, while they conversed and reasoned, that Jesus Himself drew near and went with them. (Luke 24:13–15 NKJV)

Wow, they were in difficult times, but they talked of the things of God. As they conversed, Jesus drew near. As we converse out of our fear and love of the Lord, He will draw near. After He drew near, we read, "And beginning at Moses and all the Prophets, He expounded to them in all the Scriptures the things concerning Himself" (Luke 24:27 NKJV).

What a feast! Oh, how I long to have Him revealed in a greater way. He is the satisfaction of my longing soul. As they conversed along the lines of their meditation, He drew near and opened their eyes to see Him in the Scriptures: "Then their eyes were opened and they knew Him" (Luke 24:31 NKJV). Oh, open our eyes to see Jesus, Father!

They said to each other: "Did not our heart burn within us while He talked with us on the road, and while He opened the Scriptures to us?" (Luke 24:32 NKJV). When did Moses' heart burn and his countenance change? When he heard the word of God in His presence. What gave him the ability to hear His word from His glorious presence? Moses' decision to separate from Egypt and obey the One he longed to know. He esteemed the reproach of Christ greater riches than the treasures in Egypt, for he looked to the reward. Oh, it is my hope that a longing for Him has been deeply stirred within your soul.

CHAPTER 14

They Shall See His Face

They will stand before Him free from the spots of the world, with hearts ignited with holy passion.

Our greatest days lie just ahead. God has reserved a people for Himself. They will listen for the cry of His heart and walk holy before Him. They will truly personify believers—those who hear and obey His voice without doubting. They will stand before Him free from the spots of the world, with hearts ignited with holy passion. Just as He is jealous for them, so they will be jealous for Him. Through this people, He will reveal His glory to a lost and dying world.

We find a foreshadowing of what God will do for those who honor Him in the life of Jacob, Abraham's grandson. God told Jacob: "Arise, go up to Bethel and dwell there; and make an altar there to God" (Gen. 35:1 NKJV). *Bethel* means "house of God." At another time Jacob had met with God there. God invited him, "Jacob, draw near to Me, and I will draw near to you." Jacob responded and in turn instructed his household:

> Put away the foreign gods that are among you, purify yourselves, and change your garments. Then let us arise and go up to Bethel; and I will make an altar there to God, who answered me in the day of my distress and has been with me in the way which I have gone. (Gen. 35:2–3 NKJV)

They were to "put away the foreign gods." Remember, an idol is what we give our strength or affection to, over and above Jesus. The idolatry of the Laodicean church was their covetousness, which robbed them of the necessary passion to produce eternal works (Col. 3:5). Jacob's instructions to "purify yourselves, and change your garments" reaffirmed the importance of purity and proper covering. Jesus addressed the church of Laodicea in a similar manner.

Jacob and his clan drew near to God: "And they journeyed, and the terror of God was upon the cities that were all around them, and they did not pursue the sons of Jacob" (Gen. 35:5 NKJV). The fear of God covered them to such a degree that its terror settled upon the surrounding cities they passed on their journey. When we consecrate ourselves to God, the authority of His presence accompanies us and becomes evident to those around us.

SOLD OUT TO GOD

Charles Finney was completely sold out to God. This consecration stood out above all else in his life. It rested upon him in the messages of purity he preached. For example, he visited a factory of approximately three thousand employees. The owner and most of the factory workers were not saved. Finney had been conducting a local crusade, and a woman recognized him and made a derogatory comment. Immediately, the conviction of God overwhelmed her and spread to others as they stopped their work to comfort her. Within minutes all production was brought to a halt while the workers and owner were captivated by Charles Finney's preaching of the Word of God. Within hours the majority were saved. He wore the presence of God as a garment, and it was evident to those around him, Christian and heathen alike.

Why has the church lacked the authority of this kind of presence over the last few decades? For too long the world has reviled the American church and jeered, "Where is your God?" If we have suffered persecution, it is rarely for righteousness' sake. Most often we are persecuted for our faults and worldliness. Yet I believe once again God will have a people completely consecrated to Him. My heart burns for it. Does yours? The Lord will abide with them and surround them in a powerful and obvious way. Once again the fear of God will encompass God's children as in the days of old.

Throughout this book I have referred to Moses and the children of Israel. The first generation did not forsake the desires of Egypt. However, the next generation of Hebrews had wandered through barren wastelands and consecrated themselves to the Lord. It was the generation that followed Joshua. In the book of Joshua, we find only one incident of disobedience or idolatry, which involved one family, and the nation as one rose up in opposition to it (Josh. 7).

As they prepared to cross the Jordan and face their enemies, Moses addressed them:

> Hear, O Israel. You are now about to cross the Jordan to go in and dispossess nations greater and stronger than you, with large cities that have walls up to the sky. The people are strong and tall—Anakites! You know about them and have heard it said: "Who can stand up against the Anakites?" But be assured today that the LORD your God is the one who goes across ahead of you like a devouring fire. He will destroy them; he will subdue them before you. And you will drive them out and annihilate them quickly, as the LORD has promised you. (Deut. 9:1–3 NIV)

Are we a generation like Joshua's? Are we willing to walk in such purity that God might anoint us so that the world will not overcome us? Let it be your prayer!

AN OVERCOMING CHURCH

The early church walked in the glorious presence of God. The church prayed and buildings shook. Ananias and Sapphira brought a deceitful offering before Peter and fell over dead. So evident and strong was God's presence that the Scripture records:

> But none of the rest dared to associate with them; however, the people held them in high esteem. And all the more believers in the Lord, multitudes of men and women, were constantly added to their number; to such an extent that they even carried the sick out into the streets, and laid them on cots and pallets, so that when Peter came by, at least his shadow might fall on any one of them. (Acts 5:13–15 NASB)

Not so today. Impostors easily mingle among the true because we lack the terror or fire of God. The couple's deaths alerted the surrounding society not to play games with God or His people, and multitudes came into the kingdom (Acts 5:16). Those who hungered for God recognized Him among believers, but hypocrites drew back in fear.

The early church was an overcoming church. Jesus promised the Laodicean church, so similar to ours today: "To him who overcomes I will grant to sit with Me on My throne, as I also overcame and sat down with My Father on His throne" (Rev. 3:21 NKJV).

The church that received the harshest rebuke in Revelation was also offered the greatest promise. The psalmist cried out just to be a doorkeeper in the throne room of God. Yet Jesus issued not only an invitation to the throne room, but also one to sit with Him on His throne! Perhaps now we can better understand Paul's words:

> If we endure,
> > We shall also reign with Him.
> If we deny Him,
> He also will deny us. (2 Tim. 2:12 NKJV)

How could someone who professes Jesus as Lord deny Him? We find the answer in this verse: "They profess to know God, but in works they deny Him" (Titus 1:16 NKJV). Again we see that works speak louder than confessions. Paul also encourages us, "If we endure, we shall also reign with Jesus."

Holiness involves a commitment to run to the end. We have the blessed promise that God has given us His grace that we might persevere and obtain victory! These are the overcomers, and God promises them: "They will see his face, and his name will be on their foreheads. There will be no more night. They will not need the light of a lamp or the light of the sun, for the Lord God will give them light. And they will reign for ever and ever" (Rev. 22:4–5 NIV).

Moses desired above all else to see His face. Those who overcome shall see it as they reign with Him forever and ever. You hold this book because it is your deepest desire and His greatest invitation. Embrace it, let the fire kindle, and behold Him. May the grace of our Lord Jesus abound in you. Amen.

About the Author

John Bevere is the best-selling author of several books, including *The Bait of Satan, The Fear of the Lord,* and *Thus Saith the Lord?* John and his wife, Lisa, a best-selling author as well, founded John Bevere Ministries in 1990. Since that time the ministry has grown into a multifaceted international outreach that includes a weekly television broadcast, *The Messenger.* John ministers in conferences and churches both nationally and internationally. He and Lisa reside in Colorado with their four sons.

Other Books by John Bevere

The Bait of Satan

The Bait of Satan Study Guide

Breaking Intimidation

The Devil's Door

The Fear of the Lord

Thus Saith the Lord?

Victory in the Wilderness

The Voice of One Crying

To receive JBM's free newsletter, *The Messenger,* and
to receive a free and complete color catalog, please contact:

John Bevere Ministries
P.O. Box 2002
Apopka, FL 32704-2002
Telephone: 407-889-9617
1-800-648-1477
(U.S. Only)
Fax: 407-889-2065
E-mail: jbm@johnbevere.org
Web site: www.johnbevere.org

In Europe, please contact the ministry at:

John Bevere Ministries International Ltd.
P.O. Box 138
Lichfield
WS14 OYL
United Kingdom
Telephone/Fax: 44-1543-483383
E-mail: jbeurope@johnbevere.org

The Messenger television program airs on The Christian Channel
Europe. Please check your local listings for day and time.